Andrew R. Gottlieb, PhD
Editor

Side by Side
On Having a Gay or Lesbian Sibling

More pre-publication
REVIEWS, COMMENTARIES, EVALUATIONS . . .

"**A**n outstanding contribution to LGBT family studies, *Side by Side* is the third installment in Andrew Gottlieb's trilogy of books on the relationships among gays, lesbians, and their families of origin. A work of humanity and grace, it gives a voice to the brothers and sisters of gay men and women, a group whose unique perspective has seldom been explored in print. Written by siblings themselves, the text's essays reveal the complex—and very human—issues that so often emerge among family members having dissimilar sexual orientations. From a straight man's panic at having a gay brother to a heterosexual woman's sense of confusion about her lesbian sister, the narratives further illustrate how such initial reactions may, in time, be transformed into enhanced understanding and mutual respect. Warm, insightful, and well-written, *Side by Side* is a valuable text not only for clinicians and researchers, but also for those brothers and sisters, gay and straight alike, who wish to learn more about preserving their family bonds."

Marc E. Vargo, MS
Author, *Noble Lives: Biographical Portraits of Three Remarkable Gay Men— Glenway Wescott, Aaron Copland, and Dag Hammarskjöld* and *Acts of Disclosure: The Coming-Out Process of Contemporary Gay Men*

"**B**y turns heartwarming and heartrending, *Side by Side* is a mustread for anyone who has a gay brother or sister, wonders if he or she does, or is thinking about coming out to his or her family. Gottlieb does a masterful job of presenting stories that illustrate the range of emotions that brew within the family unit: the fear of rejection, the needless regret, the yearning for understanding, and the utter joy of acceptance. If you have a gay sibling, or you've come out to your family, you'll see yourself inside these pages."

Tim Bergling
Author, *Sissyphobia: Gay Men and Effeminate Behavior* and *Reeling in the Years: Gay Men's Perspectives on Age and Ageism*

"**S**ide by Side is a collection of important and powerful stories that highlight the changes and the complexities of family life when a child 'comes out' and 'lives gay.' Each essay offers much food for thought. Some witty, some heartbreaking, all are told with candor and warmth. I was drawn into each sibling's experience and, at the end, I felt as if I were saying goodbye to good friends.

Side by Side will be required reading in my classes because, as a mental health clinician, I recognize its practical value and, as an educator, it will inevitably stimulate class discussion. For gay clients, this book offers insight, support, and understanding; for family members and practitioners, it offers the potential for developing greater awareness of and sensitivity toward others who are different. *Side by Side* is an important contribution to the field. I highly recommend it."

Dale-Elizabeth Pehrsson, EdD
Assistant Professor
for Counselor Education,
Oregon State University

Side by Side
On Having a Gay or Lesbian Sibling

HAWORTH Gay & Lesbian Studies
John P. De Cecco, PhD
Editor in Chief

Side by Side
On Having
a Gay or Lesbian Sibling

Andrew R. Gottlieb, PhD
Editor

HPP

Harrington Park Press®
An Imprint of The Haworth Press, Inc.
New York • London • Oxford

Harrington Park Press®, an imprint of The Haworth Press, Inc., 10 Alice Street, Binghamton, NY 13904-1580.

PUBLISHER'S NOTE
Some of the identities of the writers, their family members, and other individuals have been changed to protect confidentiality.

Cover design by Kerry E. Mack.

Library of Congress Cataloging-in-Publication Data

Side by side : on having a gay or lesbian sibling / Andrew R. Gottlieb, editor.
    p. cm.
   Includes bibliographical references.
   ISBN 1-56023-464-4 (hard : alk. paper)—ISBN 1-56023-465-2 (soft : alk. paper)
   1. Gays—United States—Family relationships—Case studies. 2. Brothers and sisters—United States—Case studies. 3. Coming out (Sexual orientation)—United States—Case studies. I. Gottlieb, Andrew R.

HQ76.3.U5S53 2004
306.76'6—dc22

2004004257

To my brother, Paul,
and to my father
on his 90th birthday

Since childhood, Sara and I have always had a special language. If something goes wrong, we've always asked each other to send white light. "My friend is really sick. Send white light." "You're going into surgery soon. I will send you white light." "I'm exhausted. Could you send white light?" I've come to realize Sara actually *is* white light. So am I.

How fortunate we are sisters.

Kate Boesser
"Sara and I"

I would never have known Dan was gay, even if he had leaped down the stairs and announced he had just joined the cast of *A Chorus Line* or had sewn a rainbow flag onto his cardigan. I was just two years out of high school when he told me but had been too oblivious, too preoccupied, and working too hard at a breakfast cereal corporation in Battle Creek, Michigan, to notice much of anything beforehand.

Tom Nelson
"A Lesson Learned"

Who she is has affected who I am in thousands of ways. Some of them have probably been to my detriment, but there are none that I would trade, and none that I can fully separate from the ways in which the common threads running through our early lives entwined us both.

Ann McWhorter
"Common Threads"

CONTENTS

ABOUT THE EDITOR

Andrew R. Gottlieb, PhD, is a Clinical Supervisor at the Children's Aid Society-PINS Diversion Program in Brooklyn, New York, and a private practitioner. He has published in the *Clinical Social Work Journal* and is the author of two other Haworth Press books: *Out of the Twilight: Fathers of Gay Men Speak* (2000) and *Sons Talk About Their Gay Fathers: Life Curves* (2003). Dr. Gottlieb also serves on the editorial board of the new *Journal of GLBT Family Studies.* Visit his Web site at <www.andrewrgottlieb.com>.

CONTRIBUTORS

Kate Boesser was raised in Juneau, Alaska, and educated at Middlebury College, Middlebury, Vermont; Minneapolis College of Art and Design, Minneapolis, Minnesota; the University of Alaska, Juneau, Sitka, and Fairbanks campuses; and Sheldon Jackson College, Sitka, Alaska, where she studied education, art, illustration, and writing. She has been an artist, an illustrator, a writer, a printmaker, and a wood and stone carver. Since age twenty-three, she has lived in the town of Gustavus, Alaska, with her partner and their two daughters. Currently she writes, carves, teaches art, and drives a pony that pulls an Amish wagon for tourists and weddings.

Kaye Lewis Cook graduated college in 1976 with a BS in English, and then she taught middle and high school for five years prior to her current job as a preschool teacher and supervisor. Kaye has published a few short stories and some children's literature and currently lives with her oldest daughter and their cat, Gypsy.

Terry Dolney lives on a twenty-acre forested hill near a small lake twenty miles outside of Portland, Oregon, with her husband, Ted; their son, Doug, age twenty-five, a firefighter and an emergency medical technician; and their daughter, Tianna, age twenty-four, a student studying sports massage. Their oldest, Duke, age twenty-six, is a computer geek residing in Los Angeles, California. When not working at the County Health Division in Oregon City, Terry reads, crafts, camps, and watches rodeos.

Shari Hanofee is a personal life coach, whose weekly column, "Heart to Heart" has been published in several newspapers. She holds seminars on self-acceptance, empowering women through her private life-coaching practice. She is also working on a book, titled *Throw Away Your Scale and Embrace the Power Within:*

A Journey to Self-Acceptance. Shari lives in Upstate New York with her husband and their two children.

Ariana Lee was born in New York City but has lived in Pennsylvania since she was eight years old. Now in high school, Ariana plans to attend college and major in speech-language pathology and audiology. She has never had any of her writings published before and is extremely excited about sharing her story.

Lisa B. Lewis is a variety entertainer who uses circus skills, magic, and humor. She has amused audiences in venues as diverse as King Richard's Faire, Nagasaki Holland Village, Rodeo Houston, the Michigan State Fair, Lincoln Center Out-of-Doors, and the Big Apple Circus-Clown Care Unit. She graduated from Brandeis University, Waltham, Massachusetts, with a BA in theater arts and from New York University, New York City, with an MA in clown/circus history.

Amber Hannah Love is a graduate of Skidmore College, Saratoga Springs, New York, majoring in women's studies. Currently, she is the development editor for *Expository Magazine: Feminist Literary Explorations*; a tutor; a teacher in the literacy community; and an activist for peace as well as women's and children's causes.

Luke Markert grew up in Victoria, Texas, and now resides in Corpus Christi, Texas, with his wife, Michelle, and daughter, Kathleen. His brother, John, has moved back to the United States to attend graduate school at Indiana University, Bloomington, but plans to return to Thailand after graduation to live with his partner. His parents, Ken and Linda, reside in Cuero, Texas, where they run a family business.

Ann McWhorter is an attorney in Atlanta, Georgia. Married with one daughter, she is a 1984 graduate of Birmingham-Southern College, Birmingham, Alabama, and a 1988 graduate of Harvard Law School, Cambridge, Massachusetts. Her sister, Ladelle McWhorter, is a professor of philosophy and women's studies and an author.

Tom Nelson is an information technology technician working at a corporation in Kalamazoo, Michigan, while completing a degree in creative writing at Western Michigan University, Kalamazoo.

Brad Randall received bachelor of science degrees in history and social science. Currently, he is pursuing his master's degree and is a member of both his school's Sexual Minority Student Alliance and the local PFLAG chapter.

Tess Russo lives in the Midwest with her lifetime partner of eighteen years along with their two sons. Recently, she completed an intensive training program fulfilling a lifelong dream of becoming a massage therapist.

Meredith Greenfield Siegel earned her undergraduate degree at Brandeis University, Waltham, Massachusetts, and did graduate-level studies in both elementary education and theater. Now a stay-at-home mom, she has worked as a waitress, a photo editor, a picture researcher, and an actress.

Erin Michael Starr earned her honors bachelor of science in psychology from Oregon State University, Corvallis, in 2001 and presently continues graduate studies there in the Counseling Program as well as teaches an undergraduate class. Erin spends her free time studying voice, relaxing in Oregon State's Queer Resource Center, watching *Star Trek,* and talking to her brother, John, on her cell phone. Currently she resides in Corvallis with her cat, Jiggers.

Maggi Sullivan is a rehabilitation counselor at Ontario ARC in Canandaigua, New York. Previously, she spent twelve years teaching high school and college and twenty years in the restaurant industry.

Brian Watts lives in Salt Lake City, Utah, with his wife, Kathryn Cowles. He is completing his law degree at the S.J. Quinney College of Law at the University of Utah, Salt Lake City, where he serves as executive editor of the *Utah Law Review* and is involved in the Gay and Lesbian Law Alliance. In his spare time, Brian enjoys reading and listening to music, especially Neil Young. He has been involved in several gay rights-related legal projects in both city and state politics.

Christian Webb is a 1999 graduate of Amherst College, Amherst, Massachusetts, with a degree in English. He is the founder and contributing editor of the progressive political Web-zine, Wickedphilosophy.com. His piece, "When We Were Them," about the revolving door of ethnic prejudice, appeared in the summer 2001 issue of *AIM: America's Intercultural Magazine*. Also an actor and director, Christian has appeared onstage on both coasts. He currently resides in his hometown of West Springfield, Massachusetts.

Meg Weber is a nonfiction writer whose work appears in *Sex & Single Girls: Straight and Queer Women on Sexuality* (Seal Press). She is grateful to her brother for accepting her version of this story, and to the writing itself for illuminating that she's no longer angry with her parents. Her next creative gig will be to birth and raise a child with her queer, polyamorous family of three in Portland, Oregon.

Acknowledgments

No one writes a book alone—no one. There are some who contribute directly to the finished product and some who don't, but even those who don't have an important place. They are among the people responsible for nurturing one's interests and talents.

I've been lucky over the years. I've had several people—professional mentors—who supported me and believed in me, even during those darker periods when I had serious doubts about or had stopped believing in myself. To them I am forever grateful. In that spirit, I would like to thank Phyllis Boone, Ellen Young, Michele Dubowy, and Carol Curtis.

I also feel much gratitude to my colleagues at The Haworth Press, particularly John P. De Cecco, Editor in Chief for the Gay and Lesbian Studies book program, and Bill Palmer, Publications Director. Without them, my work might never have found a home. A big thanks as well goes to the ever-dependable, ever-ready administrative and editorial Haworth "team" of (in alphabetical order): Jennifer Durgan, Dawn Krisko, Kerry Mack, Peg Marr, Amy Rentner, Josh Ribakove, Marie Spencer, Margaret Tatich, and Jason Wint.

Mention should also go to Ryan McKee, for graciously assisting with my Additional Reading list.

Above all, this book would not *be* a book without its contributors, all of whom were willing to stay with a process that was, in certain cases, emotionally quite painful. They deserve much credit.

So, to my mentors, my colleagues, and my contributors alike, I give a very warm and heartfelt thank-you.

Introduction

Andrew R. Gottlieb

In the Grimm's fairy tale "Brother and Sister" (1992), the two siblings unite. With their natural mother dead and ruthlessly beaten and starved by their wicked stepmother, they decide to leave home to begin a new life together. As they wander through the forest, the brother, after trying to restrain himself, finally drinks from a spring cursed by their stepmother after she realizes they are gone. He transforms into a fawn. Tended to by his sister, the two come upon an empty house and decide to make it their home. There they live contentedly.

One day, the king of the country decides to stage a hunt. The sounds of horns, the barking of dogs, and the excitement of the hunters all entice the little fawn. He wants to join. Reluctantly, his sister lets him, warning her brother about the brutal hunters, asking him to remember to say, "My little sister, let me in" (p. 43) as code words for her to open the door upon his return.

So fine and delicate was the little fawn that the hunters pursued him, on each successive day getting a little closer to wounding and capturing him. Finding out where the fawn and his sister live, the king himself knocks on the door of the hut and, by posing as the fawn, gains entrance. When he sets eyes on the sister, so beautiful is she, that he asks her to be his wife and live with him in his castle. She insists that the fawn live there, too. "I won't ever forsake him" (p. 44), she tells the king.

The evil stepmother, who thinks her own daughter should be married to the king, disrupts their idyllic life. Posing as a chambermaid to help take care of the queen and her newborn infant, the witch carries the queen into the bathroom, locks her in, and suffocates her to death. The witch's daughter then poses as the queen.

The spirit of the real queen returns in the night, however, looking after her baby and her fawn. The king observes her as she comes and goes, convinced that she is in fact his wife after watching her loving ministrations to their baby and her fawn. Hearing her repeatedly utter the words "How's my child? How's my fawn?" he finally exclaims, "You can be no one else but my dear wife" (p. 46). The queen magically transforms back to life, the witch and her daughter are put to death, and the fawn assumes human form. Brother and sister never leave each other "until the end of their days" (p. 46).

Throughout this story, brother and sister are inseparable: they leave home together, they live together in the forest and in the king's castle, they coexist "until the end of their days"—side by side. Although seemingly two, they are really one. Brother and sister symbolize different parts of the self. A story about growing up, the tale argues for the developmental necessity of coming to terms with the duality of our nature: the animal part of us, our id—represented by the brother/fawn—and the socialized part of us, our ego and superego—represented by the sister. All of these disparate parts of ourselves must be integrated if we are to live richly, fully, and maturely (Bettelheim, 1977). Those parts, as with siblings, are inseparable—like it or not.

Some people are struck by presence; others are struck by absence. In reviewing my own work over the past few years, it appears I fall into the latter category. My previous two books, *Out of the Twilight: Fathers of Gay Men Speak* (2000) and *Sons Talk About Their Gay Fathers: Life Curves* (2003), were born out of the belief that we lack knowledge about these experiences, with the hope that out of what was *not* would come something that *was*.

Much of the research and anecdotal literature about coming out to family members usually refers to disclosure to parents or, more recently, to spouses and children, rarely to siblings. While exploring different dimensions of the father-son relationship for my two previous books, I was impressed by the dearth of information about coming out to our brothers and sisters, even though many gay men and lesbian women disclose their sexuality to their siblings before anyone else in their families. Although those acts are significant in themselves, they frequently serve as a testing ground, safe place, or dry run before coming out to parents—an emotionally riskier endeavor. I was also struck by the fact that siblings in certain families clung to each other in order to cope with the disclosure of their father's gay identity, thus solidifying their own bond.

As clinicians, researchers, and writers, perhaps we think that the sibling relationship is not significant enough to warrant much attention. I disagree. As the stories in this anthology clearly show, finding out about one's brother or sister can be significant and life altering in its own way. Thus, out of absence comes presence— *Side by Side: On Having a Gay or Lesbian Sibling.*

The thought I had when I began this project was that editing an anthology would be easier than writing another book myself. In some ways it was, and in some ways it wasn't. In reality, it was exceedingly difficult to find enough people who not only professed an interest in contributing but also could sift through and connect with, in some instances, a difficult, traumatic past, then effectively write about those experiences, and persevere through the numerous drafts (and frustrations) to refine their stories. The majority of those who initially wrote to me about the possibility of contributing never followed through. Many I never even heard from a second time; others indicated that life circumstances—unforeseen and uncontrollable—had simply interfered. Although that may have been true, I'm also sure that it was not the only reason. Only gradually did I become aware of how emotionally difficult this assignment was for those who accepted it and, possibly, for those who couldn't.

The individuals whose stories you will read in this book are both male and female; come from eleven different states; range in age from seventeen to fifty-five years old; are straight, lesbian, and/or bisexual; and are all related by blood to their gay and lesbian siblings. Although one writer is the sister of a friend and another the sister of a man I have some acquaintance with, I had no connection whatsoever to any of the others, who were recruited from flyers I sent nationwide to Parents, Families and Friends of Lesbians and Gays (PFLAG), Children of Lesbians and Gays Everywhere (COLAGE), and the Family Pride Coalition. Six of the writers have had some of their other work published; the rest have not. All, however, have an interesting story to tell.

Christian Webb opens Part I of this anthology by wonderfully juxtaposing past and present, dreams and reality, constructing a beautifully succinct jigsaw of his experience. Ariana Lee captures how special it is to be the first in her family to know and how that served as a turning point in a brother-sister relationship that had previously never been close. Erin Michael Starr reveals that her gay half brother was the first person in her family whom she told about her *own* bisexuality, and that their unconditional acceptance of each other furthered the growing bond between them, filling in some of the missing pieces in both of their lives.

Two lesbian women, Kaye Lewis Cook, a farmer's daughter, and Amber Hannah Love, who has gone there and back and many other places, write about how having a gay brother has been a kind of anchor in the storms of their lives. Meg Weber, on the other hand, points out that being a lesbian and having a gay brother do not necessarily guarantee an intimate connection, particularly if that sibling is older and possesses a different ideological viewpoint. For her, a closer relationship with her brother, Jeff, evolved over time, so that she is only now discovering how like her brother she is.

Tom Nelson tells us about a lesson he learned; Shari Hanofee describes her older brother and his long-term partner as more than family; Lisa B. Lewis and her brother, Henry, take us down a road less traveled; and Luke Markert closes this part by reminding us that changing one's ways of thinking and being can proceed only step-by-step.

Kate Boesser opens Part II with "Sara and I," a beautifully layered account of her relationship with her activist sister. Brad Randall shatters the pact of silence in his family by speaking the evils he was not supposed to speak of. Meredith Greenfield Siegel, in rummaging through her sister's closet finds not only clothes that fit her but a closer relationship with her sister, Beth, as well. Maggi Sullivan writes about how knowing her sister, Sheila, has enriched not only her own life but the lives of her family members and others. Tess Russo expresses surprise that her own sister, the other older kid in her family, helped broaden her own concept of what it means to be lesbian, even though she herself is one. Terry

Dolney asks her half sister, Tina, to look at what she's done to help her transform her own life. Finally, Ann McWhorter poignantly weaves the ending story of this section about how common threads bind.

In the singular essay that is Part III, Brian Watts assembles the many pieces of his family puzzle, bringing the anthology itself together to a fitting conclusion.

In the film *The Perfect Son* (Jonas and Farlinger, 2002), two estranged brothers—Ryan, a successful lawyer, and Theo, an aspiring writer and recovering drug addict—are brought together by the death of their father. Opposites on the surface, they are actually more alike than they know. In a pivotal scene, when Theo goes to Ryan's home to finalize their father's will, he finds Ryan in the bedroom having sex—with another man. Theo never knew his brother was gay. A confrontation ensues:

THEO: Why didn't you tell me?

RYAN: It's just not that simple.

THEO: Oh it's not.

RYAN: No, and I didn't think you could handle it.

THEO: Why do you always talk to me like that?

RYAN: What do you mean? You could've handled it?

THEO: Yeah.

RYAN: Well then I'm an idiot.

THEO: Yeah, you're an idiot and you're a liar 'cause you didn't want Dad to know the truth.

RYAN: But you want to know the truth, do you?

THEO: Yeah.

RYAN: Alright, c'mon.

With that knowledge, Ryan seizes the opportunity to take Theo on a journey into his world, showing him who he really is, his flaws *and* perfections, leaving them both, in the end, profoundly changed, closer as brothers and as human beings.

The brothers and sisters who contributed to this book have also been affected in some ways after learning their siblings are gay and lesbian. For some, those effects have been modest, and for others, they have been profound. Although the stories speak for themselves and do not require much analysis, I am struck by one particular commonality: Almost every piece ends with an affirmation of the gay or lesbian sibling. Impressed by their siblings' courage and honesty, many of these brothers and sisters are inspired to live life the same way—side by side.

REFERENCES

Bettelheim, B. (1977). *The uses of enchantment: The meaning and importance of fairy tales.* New York: Vintage Books.

"Brother and Sister" (1992). In J. Zipes (Trans.), *The complete fairy tales of the Brothers Grimm* (pp. 41-46). New York: Bantam Books.

Gottlieb, A. R. (2000). *Out of the twilight: Fathers of gay men speak.* Binghamton, NY: Harrington Park Press.

_____ (2003). *Sons talk about their gay fathers: Life curves.* Binghamton, NY: Harrington Park Press.

Jonas, J. (Producer) and Farlinger, L. (Director) (2002). *The perfect son* [film]. Available from Wolfe Video, New Almaden, CA.

PART I:
ON HAVING A GAY BROTHER

– 1 –

Jigsaw

Christian Webb

Mom comes home early before picking Dad up from work and has that look plastered on her face that tells me I am in major trouble. She has to talk to me, seriously this time, eye to eye, with my complete attention. What have I done? I have been home from college only for two days, and the previous night's revelry with my home friends was subdued. What have I done? She pulls me away from the computer, has me shut it off, and sits me down. She smiles; she frowns. I stir; I stare. Her mouth opens.

I gazed at the story Matt had written. It was classic teen angst, and since he was hovering just past twenty, that made sense. One of the characters, Oliver, was in his late teens and going through an identity crisis. Oliver was terrified to look into the mirror to see the gay youth he was. At one point in the story, the character's name was omitted, and in its place, was the name *Matthew*. Living vicariously through the character's predicament is something writers do to help the flow of ideas. I figured Matt must have done that in this case.

"I need you to listen to me carefully. I don't know how to tell you this." By now, I'm antsy and irritated, but I can see that Mom is in no mood for attitude. I still think that I've done something, so I will not feed the fire further. "Your brother called us last night really upset. He says that he's gay."

Matt expressed his dismay to Mom that he did not want this girl to keep at him looking for a date. I lay in bed listening to the kitchen discussion, crazily jealous. Sure, I was only in sixth grade, but I had an unrequited crush on the tallest girl in class. Was I too short, too weird, too ugly? This girl was taller than Matt, and as with any normal sibling, I considered myself superior in looks and personality. All I could think was "Wow! It is possible to be liked. How could he turn her down?" He told Mom that he just wasn't ready for a relationship, and she helped him to craft a way to let the girl down easy. I told myself, "Don't be like him" because being liked is much better than being ignored. I drifted to sleep upset that Matt would pass up such a chance.

I sigh and smirk at the news. Mom searches my placid look for anxiety or confusion. The two of us are caught between generational complexities of reaction for which there is no textbook. By this point in my life, I have had several experiences with men liking or making advances toward me. Mom does not know any gay people very well. I have been mistaken for gay due to my style of dress, earring and chain adornments, and hair color changes. I've been called *faggot* while walking alone down a dark road at college, not knowing why anonymous epithets were flying my way. Mom sees that her married older son is now her gay and married older son.

Matt's wedding ended a tumultuous ten-day span during which his fiancée's dog and two of the prospective guests, one a relative, died. We all went through the yo-yoing emotions of the wake, bachelor party, funeral, rehearsal dinner, and wedding. The reception found us all cutting loose. I returned to my junior year in college and ran into someone I hadn't seen for two years. I had been a freshman then, and Matt a senior. We had known Tess socially, but separately. Tess approached me as I walked to the dining hall: "I don't want this to offend you, but I was surprised your brother got married. I thought he was gay." I didn't know how to react to this, since I was steeped in my own world of misidentification. I figured Tess's mistake would become another Webb brother trait, as are our red hair and slight builds. I told Tess that Matt definitely had his eccentricities, but that he was more akin to TV's Frasier Crane. Matt liked opera and musicals instead of sitcoms and sports, Matt liked cuisine and fancied himself a wine expert, but

Matt had always dated women and was just married. Married people aren't gay. Right?

I cannot muster more of a reaction than a quick "Okay." I really just want to get back to e-mailing my friends. I've just graduated and am preparing for my move across country to Hollywood. Long ago, I had decreed that the summer belonged to me, and now I am miffed. Is Matt's being gay that big a deal? So be it. This is a terrible inconvenience to me and my self-absorption. Me, me, me is now Matt, Matt, Matt. It won't turn back, and I now will have the task of helping those not familiar with the gay community adjust to Matt's declaration. As worldly as I find myself, even *I* need to adjust to this. Just not now.

The summer after Matt's marriage, I had an odd dream. Matt was gay and I had just found out, last among everyone we knew. My parents, grandparents, and his wife knew he was gay and it did not bother them. I was upset no one had told me sooner. I woke up and went downstairs at Matt's house. I was the last one up among my parents, grandparents, and the happy couple. I revealed my dream to the laughs of everyone. Such ridiculous thoughts! What an active imagination! Not everyone was laughing with such ease, though.

What did Dad say? "He seemed to take it in stride but was very quiet." Mom quickly shifts gears and tells me that Matt wants us to shout this from the treetops. We decide that the circumstances dictate greater discretion. Because of the disorienting news of Matt's homosexuality, we choose not to tell anyone else at the time. In recent years, much lighter issues have been treated with derision by our community. Due to academic prowess, Matt and I had experienced the scrutiny of townsfolk we did not even know. As the older sibling, Matt had the poor luck of being the first to the wolves. Matt turned down Harvard for Amherst, and we were besieged with phone calls at home and catcalls while we were out. How could he do that to this town—snub his nose at the Ivy League? We cannot see how those same people would accept the latest twist in Matt's life, and we do not want to sit around proffering explanations.

Mike was my closest childhood friend and my roommate in Hollywood. We hadn't seen each other much the summer before we convened out west. I had not wanted to tell him my brother's news over the phone. He took it well and offered support. Slowly, I revealed the news to friends I could trust. Among the group from my youth, there have always been phrases tossed around in jest that could be construed as homophobic, though a benign homophobia. Still, I did not know how exactly to reveal this without catching grief. I hoped the rumor mill would circulate so I could deal with this from afar. It did. Before I could answer the obvious question from them, I had to talk to Matt. He claimed to have known since he was eleven. It also turned out that his wife knew before they got married, but they felt they could work it out. They couldn't and Matt became single. I was relieved by this, so that he could begin to know himself as a gay man after living twenty-five years as an outwardly straight man. From California, I helped my parents to adjust to Matt's new life. They had accepted him and had never ceased to love him, but the sight of him with a guy instead of a girl was difficult to grasp.

Mom sheds a few tears, claiming she was a bad mother. I stare at her perplexed. She feels that she let Matt down, that Matt should have told her years before, that she could have made his life easier. My mind is spinning. How could she be blaming herself for any problems Matt experienced? She never would have coaxed it out of him, especially since his being gay was never suspected. I console her from across the room, not knowing what else to say.

The family has evolved since Matt's coming out. My parents took time to learn about the social and political implications of homosexuality, and I crusaded on my own among my friends to ease their uncertainties. The toughest part for Matt seemed to be that we accepted him so easily. Small confrontations would abound, but I couldn't figure out what he was fighting against. He seemed to have stored aggressive energy to embark on a fight that never happened. That has since calmed and the family has grown closer than ever.

Mom goes back to the kitchen to make dinner. I flick my computer back on. Matt and I have never been on such similar wavelengths. Yet within two days, we are both writing the first chapters of new phases of our lives.

– 2 –

I Was the First to Know

Ariana Lee

In many households, homosexuality is often looked down upon, but in my eyes, it was never a bad thing. My parents had raised us to accept everyone, no matter what their color, their culture, or their lifestyle. My mother, Anita, my father, Daniel, and I had wondered about my older brother Justin's sexuality long before it was disclosed. I don't really know if my ten-year-old sister, Chiara, had wondered too, but she had been privy to the questions we had asked about him.

Growing up, Justin and I were never really close. We played together, but we didn't have that "best friend" relationship that some siblings do. Justin was always very smart, but mostly kept to himself and never shared things with the rest of our family. He liked to read and write but wasn't very social, and he rarely talked about the friends he made. We all assumed it was a boy thing. In high school, he never really dated girls, and the relationships he had with them were never serious or long.

When I was fourteen, a freshman in high school, and Justin was seventeen, a senior at the same school, we both joined the Speech and Debate Team. We made new friends there. One person we both took a liking to was Adrian. He was an all-around, outgoing, fun person. The three of us clicked instantly. Our team was very close and it brought Justin, Adrian, and me together. Within a few months we were best friends.

Adrian began spending nights at my house and doing everything with Justin. The thought of the two of them falling for each other had crossed my mind, but I guess denial pushed that away. The absence of any real interest in girls, rare for a boy his age, always led me to question whether Justin was gay. I never disliked homosexuals or even disagreed with homosexuality before, but, subconsciously, I didn't want my brother to be gay.

The day Justin revealed his sexuality to me will probably always remain sharply etched in my mind. I had just returned home from school and things seemed tense. Something was going on. Eavesdropping, I found out the scoop. My parents were fighting with my brother and Adrian about a poem my mother came across while cleaning Justin's room. It was titled "Adrian's Song." When my mom and dad asked Justin about the poem, he told them he had written it for Lisa, a girl with whom Adrian was in love. I fell for the story—hook, line, and sinker. I think they did too. Later that night when I was lying on the basement couch watching a movie, Justin and Adrian came downstairs and looked at me in an odd way. I had a feeling they had something important to say. Little did I know my life was about to change dramatically.

Justin stood at the foot of the couch; Adrian paced back and forth. At this point I was curious. I stopped the movie and waited for one of them to say something. Then Justin began to speak: "Ariana, the poem that Mom found, that was for Adrian." Apparently Justin and Adrian felt a bit pressured to tell me this because, earlier in the day, I had passed through the room where they were watching television, and they were under the mistaken impression that I had seen them holding hands. I hadn't.

After Justin told me he was gay and Adrian was his boyfriend, I didn't know what to do or what to ask. I felt empty inside. My jaw dropped and tears started to flow like a waterfall. I wasn't angry or even upset, just in shock. I was in emotional lockdown.

After hugs all around, we sat and talked. Stumbling, I asked them questions, such as "Who's the girl in the relationship? When and how did you know you were gay?" Both of them were very understanding and patient with me. They knew they could trust me with their secret until they were ready to let the world know.

The initial shock quickly wore off. I just needed time to calm down and to understand how hard it is for some gay people to live happy lives. I felt admiration for Justin and Adrian. In my eyes they were truly courageous. I was happy for them and happy they chose to confide in me. I wasn't going to let them down.

After that night, things were uncomfortable for a while. Watching them hold hands and cuddle was strange to me. Not only had I never seen a gay couple before, but I had never seen my brother being affectionate with anyone before. I soon realized that what they had was special. Just because they were gay didn't mean they couldn't love. I felt what they felt for each other and yearned for the same. I was envious.

Before this, I had never been close with either of my siblings, and I hadn't known what it was like to have a best friend who was always there for me. After sharing his secret, however, Justin and I became best friends. Even today I tell Justin and Adrian things I don't share with others.

Sometimes, I suppose, gay people feel that if they come out, everything is going to be a mess—that family and friends will abandon them because of their own discomfort with homosexuality. In my case, however, Justin and I found a never-ending friendship. Had he not told me, we probably would not be as close as we are today.

A couple of months later, after my parents found e-mails from Adrian on Justin's computer, a crisis occurred. It wasn't up to me to say anything, so I didn't. My parents were hurt, angry, and frustrated. They had every right to be. My father was upset because Justin is the only child who could pass on our family name; my mother felt betrayed because he had lied.

Their feelings persisted for months. They tried everything—denial, blaming Adrian, not allowing Adrian in our home. When Adrian was finally allowed to visit again, he and Justin couldn't openly show affection. Things were tense around the house for some time.

My parents asked us not to talk about Justin's sexuality in front of my sister, Chiara. They felt she was too young. However, with the constant arguments between my parents and Justin, it wasn't long before Chiara figured it out. All things considered, she handled it fairly well. As with everyone else, she had questions that we did our best to answer. She cried, mostly about how her friends would hate her because her family was "weird." She was embarrassed about what everyone else would think. Chiara spoke with me the most, I think, because we were in a similar position: both girls, both Justin's siblings. She felt that, because Justin was gay, she didn't have an older brother who could defend her, and that having a gay brother was the same as having a sister. That's not abnormal for a sixth-grader, I guess.

Three years have passed since Justin came out to me. I'm seventeen years old and will be graduating high school at the end of this school year. Next year, my sister will be a freshman, the age I was when Justin disclosed to me. Chiara has now told many of her friends. When she hears the words *faggot* or *dyke,* she stands up for Justin and for herself. She now feels that having a gay brother isn't embarrassing or weird. She respects and loves Justin.

My parents have educated themselves too. They can now look at Justin and Adrian together, as a couple, and see who they truly are and what they have together. Mom and Dad sought counseling, which seemed to help.

My parents and Justin (and Adrian) are all dealing with their differences, but it's nothing but the ordinary "parent-child" issues. They have come to accept their son for who he is and have gone out of their way to show him that they are 100 percent supportive. Both my parents attend PFLAG (Parents, Families and Friends of Lesbians and Gays)—my mother started our local chapter—and GLSEN (Gay, Lesbian and Straight Education Network) meetings. Best of all, Adrian and Justin are allowed to be themselves in our house and anywhere else we go.

Justin's coming out has definitely brought us closer as a family. We have dinners and outings without the same tension. Before, when I was the only one who knew, I was watchful about what I said, careful not to reveal anything. Now I can speak freely, Justin and Adrian can be themselves, and we can even joke about it all. We've become more comfortable with homosexuality and we're spreading the word. Justin's coming out to me was the best thing that ever happened for us as brother and sister, and the best thing that ever happened for us as a family. I'm proud to have been the first to know.

3

Missing Pieces

Erin Michael Starr

If someone could have predicted five years ago that my life would be like this, I would have thought they were joking.

I grew up in a two-story white house, on a quiet street, in a small city near San Francisco. On the surface, my family appeared to others to be close to perfection. My parents were married, very much in love, and dedicated to raising their three children: the twins—Meghan and Matthew—and me. My mother had another son, Sebastian, from her first marriage. After the divorce, Sebastian lived with his father so I didn't see much of him.

Being the youngest daughter, I enjoyed the privileges that came with that position: I was rarely punished for any wrongdoings and I could take part in activities with my older siblings. I attended private schools, graduated with honors, and was actively engaged in gymnastics throughout middle school and high school. Since our city was small and my family well-known, I sometimes felt as if I were on display.

I wasn't close to either Meghan or Matthew while we were growing up, even though we were only two years apart. Meghan and I got along well enough to share our clothes, but we shared little else. She was a prominent volleyball player, and although at the top of her class, she needed to study harder than I did to get the same grades. By the time I was in high school, I attended gymnastics practice fifteen hours per week, traveling up to two hours per day, while maintaining an almost perfect grade-point average.

Most nights Meghan would already be studying when I started my homework after practice, and she would still be working after I had finished my assignments and gone to bed. Having been socialized to excel in our own individual pursuits, we often didn't have much time to be involved in each other's life.

My brother, Matthew, was a different story. I tolerated him in public, but behind closed doors he was abusive, abrasive, disrespectful, and prone to violence. When we were younger, he would try to guilt-trip me into doing what he wanted and hit me when he didn't get his way. The unspoken expectation for all of us was to project a positive image regardless of what happened at home. This made me feel as if I had to put on an act sometimes to protect everyone. I often felt isolated from my whole family, even at a young age. In my spare time, I watched television and became envious of those sitcom families, such as on *The Brady Bunch,* with characters who kept a watchful eye on their younger siblings. I wished that I had Greg Brady for a brother, someone with whom I could talk and who was supportive of my interests.

One day my wish came true.

On November 12, 2000, while attending college in Oregon, I returned to my dorm room a little after midnight. As I do every night, I decided to check my e-mail one more time while getting ready for bed. I also turned on my AOL (America Online) Instant Messenger to see who else was still awake. As I slid into my chair after changing into my pajamas, a message window opened on my computer screen:

HIM: Sorry to bother you. Are you from the Bay Area?

ME: Yup.

HIM: Wow. I think I might know who you are.

ME: Let's start with who you are.

HIM: Do you have an older brother named Matthew?

ME: Again who are you?

HIM: If you are who I think you are, it might really freak you out.

ME: Why is that?

HIM: Because you may or may not know that you have an older brother.

ME: So who are you again?

HIM: My name is John, not that it would mean anything to you though.

ME: Then why might this "freak me out"?

HIM: Because if Jennifer is your mother, then we are related.

ME: How is that?

HIM: Because she is my mother.

My jaw hit the ground: I had another brother? This happens only on *Montel Williams* or *Oprah*. Could my mother have had another child and not told us? His story sounded plausible: John was fourteen years older than I was, and he had been given up for adoption because, in the 1960s, it hadn't been socially acceptable for unmarried women to have children. I still thought it could be a hoax, so I started to quiz him on family history: names, birth dates, marriages. He knew most of the answers. In fact, he knew some things I didn't know. I figured this guy was either crazy and had put way too much effort into digging through public records or he was telling the truth. John had had his adoption and birth records opened in 1992 and had been looking for his biological family ever since. I was giddy with excitement. He seemed to be a genuine, caring man who only wanted to know his roots. I was so excited to learn about him. We talked until 4:30 that morning, and when we signed off, I saved the text of our conversation. Even now when I read it, I get tears in my eyes, still overjoyed to have John in my life.

A few hours later, I made one of the most difficult phone calls ever: I called my mother to ask if what John had told me was true. I had to push her about it, but, finally, she confirmed that John was, indeed, my half brother. She didn't want to have anything to do with him and didn't understand why I did. She wouldn't tell me why she wasn't interested in reuniting with John, but she knew that she couldn't do anything to stop me from developing a relationship with him.

John and I continued to chat over the Internet on a regular basis. We had twenty-one years of catching up to do. I glowed with happiness every time I spoke to him or about him. We often discussed how and when we might meet, since we lived almost 700 miles apart and both had busy lives. We also wondered why our mother felt so strongly against having him in her life. My theory is that when John's adoption records were sealed, she sealed off that chapter of her own life. John entering *my* life must have brought up a lot of guilt and shame—feelings she would need to make peace with before she could consider having a relationship with him.

During our chats, John and I tried to figure out what we had in common, so that when we actually did meet we would have something to do. I mentioned that I liked to go dancing with my friends and he said that he liked to do the same. Since he was still in the Bay Area, I shared that I had heard the best dancing was in the gay clubs. He agreed with me—which I didn't expect. This was the first time I thought he might be gay. I assumed that he would say he'd heard about that but had never experienced it himself, but instead he said, "It's funny you brought that up, because I am gay." I burst out laughing and responded, "I knew it!" He started laughing too. This was the icing on the cake: an awesome brother with whom I could share anything and everything *and* watch boys with too!

I was excited when John shared that he was gay. I first learned what that meant at around age twelve when I saw Pedro and Sean on MTV's *The Real World.* Since then I have been very comfortable around homosexuals. I thought two guys openly showing affection for each other was adorable. I also liked the feeling I experienced when I could talk to a guy and not have any sexual tension get in the way.

Finally, John and I were united a few months later in San Francisco Airport. I had a one-night layover and asked him to pick me up. As I walked into the terminal around nine that evening, I immediately spotted him in his orange shirt, hanging back a little from the rest of the crowd, waiting. Our eyes met and we knew. I walked up and wrapped my arms around his neck. In some ways it felt familiar to hug this person I had never seen before. A void was filled when I was finally able to touch him; that's when he truly became real. He took my bag and we started walking out of the terminal. After about ten steps, we stopped and looked into each other's eyes. They matched.

John drove me to my hotel, where we talked until almost one in the morning about where we came from—his past, my past. I felt comfortable sharing my darker side with him. I did not worry about presenting a tarnished view of the family because our mother had rejected him already. I felt I owed it to him, and to myself, to be completely honest and not project a false image. It was just as important for him to see me and accept me for who I was as it was for me to see him and accept him for who he was. John had embraced being gay years before we met, which made me feel comfortable in his presence. It was liberating to be accepted by him and to be accepting of him.

John's sexuality was never an issue for me, so it felt natural for us to watch men together. Once, while we were having burgers at Johnny Rocket, a 1950s-style restaurant, we both thought our waiter, who couldn't have been older than nineteen, was adorable. We spent the majority of the time watching his mannerisms and debating whom he was more likely to date.

The one thing I've tried to become more aware of is the stereotypes I have about others, especially homosexuals. John fits some of them, the most obvious one being his enjoyment of shopping. Once, after I made a reference to Barbra Streisand, he was quick to remind me that all gay stereotypes were just that—stereotypes—and not all of them applied to him. John exudes confidence in himself and does not conform to what other people think he should be.

Since John and I are on the same e-mail server, I check his online profile from time to time to see what he wants other people to know about him, as he changes it periodically. A little more than a year ago, I noticed a "+" at the end of the section in which he described himself as a gay man. I didn't know what it meant, so I asked him. He responded that it was a symbol for "positive." "HIV positive?" I wanted to know. "Yes," he answered. I was shocked. I felt the color drain out of my face and my heart sink in my chest. At that moment he was no longer my dependable big brother who gave me good advice. He was my brother who was going to be taken away from me by an incurable virus.

I spent the following weekend in a daze. Every other thought was, "My brother has HIV and he's going to die." Myriad feelings overwhelmed me: I felt as if someone had stabbed me in the stomach and was twisting the knife every time I had that thought; I was worried there wouldn't be time for him to be reunited and accepted by the rest of the family; I was angry at the world for bringing this wonderful person into my life and now taking him away; I was scared he was going to get sick and I would be helpless to change it; I felt selfish for having these feelings about how I was going to deal with his illness instead of focusing on his needs.

It took about a week for reality to sink in: John had been HIV positive for over ten years; his viral load was undetectable; he seemed to be on a medication regimen that was working for him; and he wasn't taking thirty pills a day. He was probably healthier than I was and happy to have me in his life.

Finding out that John has HIV has given me a sense of urgency and a stronger desire one day to see him welcomed into our family. There is nothing I can do to change people's perspective about him, but I continue to wish that they will come around and that John will continue to be as healthy as he has been. He and I have had many discussions about being gay and having HIV, and specifically what it is like for him to tell new people, especially potential partners, about his health status. I wasn't aware of the many stereotypes I held about people with HIV until I caught myself making assumptions. I thought that everyone who was infected was often sick and susceptible to illness, on a drug regimen that required over twenty pills per day, and not dating or having a love life. I feel fortunate that John is open to talking about his health and about the possibility that this disease might kill him. I find strength in his attitude. He tries to live each day to the fullest, and he's grateful he's been healthy thus far.

Our mother has voluntarily mentioned John's name three times since she found out I was spending time with him. Each time gives me hope that she will eventually accept him, at least as a part of my family if not hers. My father has known about John for a long time and supports my mother's decision not to talk to him. She explained the situation to my other siblings, none of whom have made any effort to learn more about John or to contact him. John and I accidentally ran into Sebastian and Matthew once while he was visiting my hometown. It was a short, awkward conversation, and we have never spoken about it since. Meghan told me she wants nothing to do with John out of respect for our mother. I do not think John will become accepted by anyone else in the family unless our mother accepts him first.

It angers me that they reject him without giving themselves a chance to know him. Their lack of acceptance leaves me feeling as if I live a double life—I simultaneously do and do not care what they think about my relationship with John.

Because of our relationship, I now wear the "Until There's a Cure" bracelet on my wrist to show support for HIV/AIDS research. Our mother knows that I wear it because someone close to me has the virus, but she doesn't know that it's her son and I don't think that it's my place to tell her. I want her to accept John because of who he is, not because he is HIV positive.

I feel as if I finally have the big brother I've always wanted. Sometimes I forget he's a blood relative because I'm used to being closer to my friends than to my family. With my parents and my other siblings, I monitor myself in order to stay in their good graces, given the expectation to conform to the family's perfect image. I have an irrational fear that my family will reject me if I bring up certain subjects which make them uncomfortable. John, however, accepts me unconditionally. I know I can count on him—day or night—if I want his advice or just need a sounding board.

It was relatively easy for me to come out to him as bisexual a few months ago. I had been trying to ignore my feelings, but they wouldn't go away. At the time I knew I wasn't straight, but I didn't know what to call myself when I initially told him. John just smiled and said, "I'll call you Erin," approaching my process with the same understanding and compassion he approached his own.

I was proud to introduce John to my friends during my school's Siblings' Visit. I find it amusing when those friends, who have met John and know about the missing pieces he fills in my life, spend time with my parents, who call Sebastian "the oldest." I giggle when I take day trips to see John while staying with my parents because I can say only that I'm going to visit "a friend," not that I'm going to visit John. But I know they know.

Sometimes I get upset when I think about John dying. I worry that someday I'm going to be sitting on his bed, holding his hand, and watching him deteriorate. I imagine going to his memorial service and not being able to tell my family he's dead, never having a chance to share with them what a wonderful son and brother they had and how he has enriched my life.

John said that, after he dies, he wants his family and friends to throw a party and celebrate instead of staging a dreary funeral. He thinks it's morbid to bury him or even have a place where his loved ones can "visit," preferring to be cremated and have his ashes scattered at the beach. About a year ago, I called John and admitted that, as much as I wanted to honor that request, I probably couldn't. I told him I would be tempted to return to the beach where his ashes were whenever I thought about how much I missed him. He was gentle and understanding about my fears because he knows it took a lot of courage for me to admit this. He told me to scatter his ashes from a boat on the Pacific Ocean instead, and that way if I ever needed to "visit," I could go to any beach that borders it.

After watching the movie *And The Band Played On* (1993), which chronicles the AIDS epidemic since its beginnings, I asked John if I could immortalize him on the AIDS Quilt. I cry when I watch that movie and think about how the names on those panels symbolize real people—people who were special and whose lives are remembered in this special way. He told me if he died of complications due to AIDS, I could contribute a panel in his memory. I don't know if a three-by-six-foot panel can fully express the enormity of his impact on my life, but I am eternally grateful for this shining light I call my brother.

REFERENCE

Sanford, M., Pillsbury, S. (Producers), and Spottiswoode, R. (Director) (1993). *And the band played on.* Available from HBO Video, New York, NY.

4

A Farmer's Daughter

Kaye Lewis Cook

I was born in 1951, one of nine siblings: a brother, seven years older, and seven others, all younger. Derek, my gay brother, born in 1960, is the youngest.

We grew up in rural Hoke County, fifteen miles or so from Fayetteville, North Carolina. Our father was a farmer. He grew spring, summer, and fall vegetables on a 100-acre farm, then "trucked" them to supermarkets in Fayetteville, where owners purchased his crops. As young children, much of our time was spent playing around the barn, the orchard, or the woods surrounding the fields. As we got older, by eleven or twelve, we were all expected to pitch in, especially during the summer harvest. Sometimes it was hot, but my father never allowed us to work outside during the afternoon hours because of the extreme heat. My memories of those times are good ones. We were poor, but our parents loved us very much.

I always thought of Derek as the baby and felt love and respect for him. He was cute and the youngest, so I spoiled him. So did everyone else. In a way, our parents spoiled all of us—not with money or possessions, but with caring and concern. My mother always told me that all children were different and, therefore, needed different things. She did a fine job of trying to understand her children as separate people.

I found out about Derek's sexuality around the time I acknowledged my own. About eight years ago, I was at our mother's house and he saw me reading a gay newspaper. He asked me if I was gay.

I said yes. He told me he was gay also. We were both surprised—to say the least.

At that point in time, I was forty-three, married for thirteen years, the loving mother of three small children, the devoted wife of Ernest, a man I truly cared for, and a member of the Baptist Church. My husband worked as a real estate agent and I stayed home with the kids. We lived in a peaceful suburb, not far from Fayetteville, close to both of our families. After much self-reflection and soul-searching, I realized I was a lesbian. I never really dated as a teen and, in my twenties, had a strong attraction to women but truly believed I could choose not to be gay. I lived a lie for years and could do it no longer.

One night, I acknowledged to Ernest that I was gay. At first he didn't seem that concerned and suggested I think more about it. We talked about seeing a therapist and, eventually, we did—both as a couple and individually. Days, weeks, and months passed. I grew more frightened and more confused, terrified of the possibility of losing my husband and, perhaps, my children. He started to instigate fights, demanding that I forget about this "foolishness" and get back to "normal." He was almost always angry and, at times, used violence to try to convince me to "be reasonable." Although he never struck me, he did push me around and left bruises on my arms and neck. He threw furniture, yelled, put his fists through the walls, and threatened to kill me. Our young children would be awakened in the middle of the night by his yelling and my crying. During that time, my contact with anyone except for Ernest was minimal. Even though Derek and I lived in the same community, I rarely saw him or the other members of my family.

The pressure became so great that, after a year, I moved out of the house without the children. Ernest refused to allow them to go with me. They cried. So did I. I moved in with my parents, and eventually all of our friends found out about my sexuality and our domestic problems. The pastor tried to counsel us, but after a year and a half, he kicked me out of the church, and, to my dismay, all my "friends" deserted me too. It still hurts. But I can now see that they had to make a choice, and in a rural Southern Baptist church, it would have been unpopular to support a member who had come out as a lesbian.

I never went back to Ernest. We lived apart for a year, then he filed for divorce, which I did not contest. He kept the children, but we shared joint custody. I have visitation rights and will pay child support until they each turn eighteen. I regret all our pain and suffering, but it was inevitable. I do not feel I could have lived the rest of my life denying who I was.

After I came out, Derek assured me he would always be supportive. He has kept his word. I, in turn, am supportive of him. I have accepted my sexuality, and even though it has been difficult, I live one day at a time, just as others, gay or straight, do. Life has challenges for us all, and being gay sometimes adds to the pile. At age fifty-one, however, I take it in stride. The shock and emotional trauma I dealt with was eased by Derek's disclosure and helped me in many ways. My coming out, superimposed on his, gave that whole two-year period a surreal, dreamlike, almost nightmarish quality. People were shocked by my disclosure, as they were by his; friends and family alienated me, as they did him. At least *he* understood and accepted me; at least *I* understood and accepted him. I applaud his bravery; I applaud my own.

Derek disclosed that he had known about himself since childhood. At twenty-one, he married a girl he had been going out with since age fourteen; they have two sons together and have been separated for about fifteen years. He always appeared to be straight, but, then again, so did I.

My father, now deceased, "knew" about Derek as a teenager, but never openly expressed his knowledge to anyone—except my mother. She told me that Dad once said, "Derek doesn't care for women." I don't know what he based that on, but I recall that, always a quiet, reserved man, he once said, "You can know all you want to know about people if you watch them." I guess he had been watching Derek. (Had he been watching me too?) I suppose he thought Derek's sexuality was his own business. Mom was silent as well until Derek and I both came out. She admitted at the time that she did not understand much about being gay but loved us as much as always and wanted us to be happy. Now she is extremely supportive.

Some of our siblings are a different story. Three of them have expressed disapproval of our "lifestyle"—not directly to us, but by making comments to others. As a family we tend to be non-confrontational about some issues, very open to dissent about others, and civil to one another when we are all together. Isn't life tough enough without tearing one another down? One of my brothers, Thomas, died from cancer in 2001, so perhaps our family has learned not to take relationships for granted. Thomas was probably the most openly supportive of Derek and myself, and I am touched by his devotion whenever it crosses my mind.

I have a loving relationship with my son and two daughters. The oldest moved out of her father's house and into mine on her eighteenth birthday four months ago; my sixteen-year-old son and thirteen-year-old daughter continue to live with their dad, his wife, and his wife's son. All of my children have concerns about me being a lesbian. While the older two at least acknowledge that I have a right to be who I am, the youngest does not approve and will not hesitate to voice her opinion. As a family, we are still growing, and even though they feel uncomfortable with my sexuality, I have no doubt they love me and realize that I love them too.

My life is inextricably woven into the fabric of Derek's; our relationship has always been a loving and affectionate one. Although the age difference put some distance between us when we were younger, we are now closer than ever. As a boy, he was cheerful and playful; as a teenager, I liked photography and was the family shutterbug. When Derek was five or six, I photographed him outside as he played. As young adults we partied together at times, smoking pot and drinking. Now in middle age, I feel even closer to Derek knowing he is gay. I have an ally.

Some of the issues I face are, in many ways, unlike his. He has been living with a partner for about ten years. I am now single, having been in only one two-year relationship with someone who lived four hours away from me at the time. Neither of us were willing to move, so I broke it off. I have dated lots of other women but have not yet found "Ms. Right." Being a preschool teacher and living alone sometimes makes for financial hardships, something with which Derek need not concern himself.

Besides those worries, Derek and I do face similar problems. Being gay is a pain in the ass in this straight world, and I am angry about the inequality that pervades our society. Gays, lesbians, bisexuals, and transgender citizens deserve the same rights as others, but, as of yet, we do not have them.

Would my relationship with Derek be different if one or both of us were not gay or lesbian? I cannot answer that. It *is* interesting that we both came out, unknowingly, to other family members only a few weeks before we came out to each other. I disclosed to Ernest first; Derek disclosed to Mom first. Since Ernest's response was angry and threatening, I did not want to risk getting a second helping of that from anyone. Even now, eight years later, I am careful whom I tell. This is not a gay-friendly world that we live in.

5

There and Back

Amber Hannah Love

I have known the privilege of a life lived outside the margins, a life intelligible beyond the small circle of family, friends, and mentors who have known and cared for me. One form that privilege has taken is the freedom to speak in ways not deemed acceptable in certain places. My brother, Joshua, has been my inspiration. He introduced me to so many new ways of thinking and expanded my world to include new writers, filmmakers, artists, theater, music, even new foods. My relationship with him has forever altered the ways I use language and imagery. Always a critical mentor, he has encouraged me to write, a childhood passion of mine that in adulthood has infiltrated every corner of my being.

Another of those privileges I experienced long before Joshua did was immunity in the academic arena. There I was safe from retribution, safe to speak my mind, and safe from other students. Even during the worst periods when I, myself, faced harassment, I could go there and be accepted. Outside of the classroom, however, I was called "freak," "faggot," "child of dykes," "sister of the fag," "the niece of a queer."

Because I passed for straight, I was given the privileges afforded to a heterosexual white female. For many years, I was in the closet, out only to some friends and in the community near my hometown where I was socially active. Even my family did not know I was "one" until years later.

For a time, we maintained a facade: Mom was heterosexual, divorced, and raising two children with her "best friend" Sue. The reality was that my moms were, and still are, *soul mates.* I've known that since I first heard and understood the term. When I was in high school, Mom and Sue came out. They had waited years to disclose because, in our community, job security and custody were easily jeopardized. In my own limited way, I understood that their relationship was similar to the one my Uncle Pat had had with his partner. I had heard the term *lesbian* used as a curse word and as a devaluation of women, but nothing seemed wrong about their relationship. As a child, I didn't think of my moms as lesbians, but I knew they loved each other. This past summer they celebrated their twenty-third anniversary together. My older brother, Joshua, or "Bubbalicious," is gay. Then there's me—a single, Jewish, feminist lesbian, now completing my education.

I've tried to recall when I became aware of Joshua's homosexuality. Although I cannot pinpoint what age I was, I know it was long before he actually came out to me. There was no single, revelatory moment. There were, however, many moments that underscored the difference in his outlook and preferences. He liked to make costumes and create hairstyles for my dolls, sometimes to my dismay. His preference for the arts over sports had specific meanings. In our neighborhood, playing football and baseball were measures of boyhood and precursors to manhood. His flare for fashion and theater was obvious, even though he did play a season of football and was a Boy Scout for one year. I was not a Girl Scout or much of an athlete either, even though I played soccer, softball, and golf at certain times in my life. As a young teenager, while I was considered asexual, which took some of the pressure off, my brother had the opposite problem; he was perceived as hypersexual.

Joshua came out to Mom when he was about fifteen. He then moved to Santa Fe to attend a school for the gifted and disclosed to me through a letter—a very courageous act. I was still miserable back in west Texas, living with Mom and Sue, and spending as much of my time as possible buried in a book. I had discovered my attraction to women and decided not to talk about it until I was older.

As I began exploring my sexuality, I experienced homophobia, this time directed at me. I did not want to come out fully and thus further complicate my family's life. I made that decision on my own, but it was one that, unintentionally, created another layer of secrecy and distance among all of us, even though it had seemed the best thing to do at the time.

While I was still closeted, my family referred to me as their very own Marilyn, the teenager from the TV sitcom *The Munsters*. I was the straight, supportive, feminist daughter/sister. During this period, as I have mentioned, most people thought of me as asexual. At thirteen, I knew that mine was an entirely different reality.

In September 2001, Joshua told me that he was HIV positive. Our Uncle Pat had died from AIDS in the late 1980s. I grieved for both of them. All I could think about was that Joshua was my only sibling, and that I didn't want to lose another family member to this disease. The agony I witnessed Mom going through, first watching her brother die and then fearing that the same thing might happen to her son, hit me full force. Might the day come when I would witness my only sibling in the same predicament? All of it was too much for me to handle. I emotionally shut down.

This was only the most recent crisis Joshua has faced in his twenty-eight years. There were others before it. Shortly after our Uncle Pat died, Joshua, then fifteen, attempted suicide. He was in the ninth grade and I was in the sixth, attending the same middle school from which he had just graduated. All I kept thinking was, "No, this is not happening, not to Joshua, please not to Joshua. Take it back. I can't bury my brother before he's forty, as Mom did with Uncle Pat."

I was subjected to other kids gossiping about "fags" and suicide. Some termed it *natural selection.* I wanted to believe they didn't know I was Joshua's little sister. I was used to being called "faggot lover," "dyke," or "daughter of lesbos," and I was determined that none of them see how much their words hurt me. Though I was convinced his suicide attempt was my fault, I was also aware that it was related to how he was being treated at school. Clearly his history parallels those of many other gay and lesbian adolescents. Ultimately, for me, Joshua's suicide attempt deepened my sense of wanting to work toward improving social and systemic inequalities in whatever ways I could.

More recently, Joshua fought drug addiction. So many times we thought we would lose him. I clearly remember when he came to my home during a period when he had been actively using. After he left, I sobbed for hours because I did not know how many recoveries he had left in him. His body was ravaged. I could see his pain and the distance the drugs had created between him and the rest of us. I knew if he chose to live, it would be a choice he would have to make on his own.

In different ways, I, similar to Joshua, had gone too far over the edge. I self-mutilated and was diagnosed with anorexia nervosa, all stemming from a long history of physical and sexual abuse perpetrated by distant relatives. I had stopped living, unsure if there would be a tomorrow. Through my treatment, however, I started to learn to be more present, although, in the beginning, I could manage only a few moments at a time. Eventually, days would go by when I wouldn't even think about the issues that had haunted me. To watch the brother I loved go through a similar process was often agonizing. Joshua entered inpatient rehabilitation and now attends AA (Alcoholics Anonymous) and NA (Narcotics Anonymous). On March 28, 2002, he celebrated one year being clean and sober. For both of us, it's still one day at a time.

As two young gay and lesbian kids making our ways in the world, I always wondered if the experiences Joshua and I had were similar. Since he left home during his midadolescence, we both felt as if we were the only child in our family. As adults, although we have begun to reconnect with each other, so much has been lost and yet there is still so much to discover.

Many people viewed Joshua and I as complete opposites throughout childhood. He was inevitably cast as the sun, I as the moon, reflected in our childhood nicknames, Tigger and Eeyore. We bickered in those early years because it was safest to work out with each other those hard-to-name conflicts we experienced separately and together. Some of our arguments were about fighting over our moms' attention; some were over where to eat, what movie to see, what activity to engage in—all pretty typical, I guess. Despite the conflicts, when Joshua left home, I was bereft.

My sense of loss was profound. I believed we would never live together again, and I was right.

I have wonderful memories of visiting him during Pride Week in the summers, attending the parades, the drag shows, "gay day" at a regional amusement park, as well as passing out condoms and safer-sex literature. I also remember learning about acts of hate Joshua had experienced as a teenager. Every insult and injury to him has made me more politicized, more determined to figure out ways to make a difference so that no one will have to go through what he did.

You hear people say they would go to hell and back for someone they love. Both Joshua and I think of hell as a place created by people on this planet. We've both been there and have now come back to find each other as siblings and friends. Indeed, our entire family has found one another, separately and together. We are now committed to living our lives openly, with integrity, and out of the closet, creating that privileged space for us finally to be together and "out" about all of those issues from our pasts that kept us apart unnecessarily for so long.

6

Like My Brother

Meg Weber

I wonder if my mom knew where that conversation was headed. Did she intend to out my brother in the midst of our argument, or did it slip out accidentally? If it weren't for that shirt, she might never have told me at all.

I was sixteen years old and we were shopping for school clothes before my junior year at Central Catholic High School. The shirt in question was flannel, in earthy brown and plum tones, and it fit perfectly. It was the only thing I really wanted. It was also the one thing my mother refused to buy me. Exasperated, she insisted, "It's too masculine. Why can't you dress like a girl?" In vain I tried to explain to her that I chose my clothing on the basis of comfort, not gender. At the time we probably both knew this wasn't the whole truth.

I knew the shirt itself was not the issue. It merely cloaked the heart of the problem: my mother's fear. In a trembling voice, my mother asked me if I was a lesbian. Now it was my turn to be exasperated. I wasn't offended at her accusation; I was mad because she had turned my simple longing for the perfect shirt into a much bigger issue. I replied that I was not a lesbian, defiantly adding that it wouldn't bother me if I were.

The next words out of my mother's mouth were a reluctant confession that my eldest brother, Jeff, was gay, confirming an unspoken assumption I had made years before. The shame my mother felt about Jeff being gay was palpable, overtaking her entirely. She was Catholic guilt incarnate, blaming herself for Jeff turning out "that way," and bracing herself to claim responsibility for my sexuality as well. Clearly, one of my mother's worst fears was that I, too, would turn out homosexual. For her, the only fate worse than having one of her eight children be homosexual was to have more than one be that way. I don't think she believed me when I told her I wasn't lesbian. (Fear or not, I can't fault her logic: a daughter who isn't dating; wears mostly jeans, men's flannel shirts, and Birkenstocks; plays on the high school golf team; and has intensely intimate "friendships" with women is prime lesbian material.) We were silent the rest of the way home. Neither one of us knew what else to say.

Finding out that my brother was gay was a strange sort of victory to me. It gave the ongoing battles with my parents another dimension. I could fight with them about issues of prejudice, shame, and oppression without being the focal point of the argument. Later that year when Jeff got a boyfriend, constant tension between Jeff and my parents surrounded family events. My mother made arbitrary decisions about which gatherings Jeff's boyfriend could attend and which he could not. It was my voice that protested this injustice, not my brother's. Unlike Jeff I would not concede to my mother's whims. I continually challenged her on statements loaded with prejudice, such as, "If only he [Jeff's partner] didn't look so obviously gay, then when they went out in public no one would know." This verbal battling characterized my arguments with my parents amid the incessant push-pull of struggling for my independence from them. I was still unwilling to focus on my own sexual self, but it was blatantly obvious where my allegiances stood.

My commitment to fighting my parents' discrimination was more about my own personal war with them than about standing up for my brother. Sure, I was looking out for Jeff, but not out of some deep-seated kinship he and I shared. I spoke out because I was angry at my parents. At that point in my life, I hardly knew my brother. He's thirteen years older than I am and was already out of the house before I was old enough to know him well. While I was in high school, he spent three years living in Hawaii and I saw him about once a year. We were strangers to each other. I know I assumed he was gay, but looking back now, I am not sure why. I knew he wasn't the same as my four other brothers, all of whom are athletic and competitive and sarcastic. Jeff is different, quieter, and definitely more private than the rest of my family. I knew he'd never had a girlfriend. It just wasn't something that was talked about; it was one more layer in our big Catholic family of secrets and lies.

It wasn't until years later that I began to have any real relationship with Jeff. When I was a freshman in college, I came out to myself and everyone in my life (except my parents) as bisexual. I made a point of telling Jeff, hoping to forge a deeper bond via our shared experiences of being gay. The problem was that we had no common ground. He was a closeted, highly conservative, Republican gay man, and I was a young, vocal, political, radical dyke. I had more in common with my progressive straight friends than I did with my gay brother. It was disillusioning and ironic. My mother had been so afraid that I would end up "like my brother," and yet, although I did end up queer, I was, in actuality, not similar to him at all.

When I finally came out to my parents, having a gay sibling didn't provide the oasis of support one might expect. Jeff's coming out barely paved the way for me because I wasn't as willing to acquiesce to my parents as he was. Although it was definitely a struggle for my parents to accept their gay son, the process was made easier by Jeff's closeted existence. My outspoken, defiant views on sexuality seemed to make Jeff as uncomfortable as it did my parents, which I hadn't expected. The deafening indifference of my other siblings didn't bother me as much as the lack of support I felt from my gay brother. I somehow expected our choice of same-sex partners to create an alliance between us.

That spontaneous connection never happened. Instead, Jeff and I have each worked at opening up to each other over the past few years. Looking back on my mother's confession about Jeff, I am grateful to her for telling me the truth. At the time, I was probably more interested in that flannel shirt than in a relationship with a brother I hardly knew, but I believe that conversation laid the groundwork for Jeff and I to form the relationship we have today.

In many ways, I consider him my closest sibling, something I never would have expected eleven years ago when I first found out he was gay. Together we are finding ways to bridge the chasms of our age difference and disparate experiences of being queer.

7

A Lesson Learned

Tom Nelson

I would never have known Dan was gay, even if he had leaped down the stairs and announced he had just joined the cast of *A Chorus Line* or had sewn a rainbow flag onto his cardigan. I was just two years out of high school when he told me but had been too oblivious, too preoccupied, and working too hard at a breakfast cereal corporation in Battle Creek, Michigan, to notice much of anything beforehand. I wasn't the only one. We were *all* oblivious—Mom, Dad, and I.

At age nineteen, Dan was simply not transparently gay. He was a year and a half younger than I, but we enjoyed many of the same things: action movies and music—punk, heavy metal, and hard rock. Girls loved him, not because he was a shoulder to cry on, but because he was a handsome man with a sense of humor, though sarcastic: "Your ego-fascist mother looks great in curlers" or "Can't you pick out some music not worth strangling ourselves over" were typical comments. It just wasn't something I saw coming.

As a typical, Midwestern, heterosexual male, I thought being gay meant you had to be effeminate, wear leotards, or teach aerobics. I was ignorant. What I could never have anticipated was that I, too, would feel, not the same, but a pain similar to that which Dan hid and endured for years. Despite my ignorance, I eventually came to understand my brother, myself, and the world a little bit better.

The night Dan decided to disclose to me, we were together—as always—at a party where all our friends were drinking malt liquor and playing video games. I was smoking a cigarette out on the porch and, like a crude, sex-deprived convict, I said, "Damn, you know, that Samantha chick is hot. Her tits are like Florida oranges." My brother simply grunted as if he were mildly amused or offended by my comment. It was an ambiguous grunt, which became characteristic of him when he had to listen to others talk about their sexual liaisons or inquire if he had a new girlfriend he was "trying to pin on the ropes." Besides being annoyed by my insensitivity, Dan just wasn't his chipper, cynical self. As I was nudging his elbow about Samantha, he was probably trying to work up the courage to disclose his sexuality to the person who had been in his life the most—me.

After my friends passed out, my brother and I managed to make it back home and into our beds—two singles on either side of the room, which at first glance, resembled Beaver and Wally Cleaver's bedroom. Ours, however, was cluttered with Dan's heavy metal skeleton posters, a battered guitar, and an amplifier. I closed my eyes, feeling black-and-blue from drink, until my brother startled me.

"Dude"—the kind of "Dude" that easily substituted for "Listen"—ever-cryptic teen talk.

"Yeah, dude?"

"I've gotta tell ya something."

"All right."

"I've been thinking 'bout something I want to tell you. You're not going to freak out or anything?"

"What is it?"

"Just don't get mad—promise?"

"I won't. What?"

"Remember when you said a couple months ago about those two guys, Jimmy and Tim, that—"

"The gays?"

"Jimmy and Tim, that you respected them because they were public and shit, and they were brave, kinda like black people during the fifties?"

"Yeah."

Months prior, I had been introduced to a gay couple for the first time. Although apprehensive at first, eventually I had accepted their differences and befriended them. I had told my brother that I thought their struggle was similar to that of black Americans during the 1950s, but instead of being blasted with a fire hose or made to sit at the back of the bus, Jimmy and Tim were forced to conceal their love from plaid-shirted rednecks.

"Do you still believe that?"

"Yeah."

"Because I just wanna make sure you're okay with it."

"With what?"

"I'm gay."

My brother told me the one secret he had kept buried under hundreds of heavy metal songs and guitar notes. At first, it seemed as if a blast of air from the open bedroom window had uttered the phrase *I'm gay.* But no.

"What?"

"I'm gay"—this time said threateningly, suggesting that I had better not laugh or, worse yet, run away.

A tear fell onto my pillow that night, the only one I will ever shed for my brother's homosexuality. Not that I don't care. I do. But when I imagine Dan fighting the fire hose or those plaid-shirted bigots of discrimination as a fearless leader championing equality, the sadness inevitably stops and becomes admiration.

"It's . . . it's okay."

"It is?"

"Yeah, you're my bro'. I don't care if you are gay, you'll still be my bro'."

I still am and always will be his brother whether he likes men, women, or three-eyed aliens. My parents responded differently. Dan told me that he had become aware of feeling attracted to guys at around age sixteen. Those feelings had percolated for three years until he finally disclosed to Mom. She had wept, not out of shame or disappointment, but out of not being able to protect him. He told me a day later. My dad, the last to know, felt responsible and guilty and wondered if he should have painted Dan's room blue instead of yellow or taught him to play football instead of letting him play guitar. Eventually, we all learned to keep our private worries out of the way and to concentrate on Dan.

For me, my brother's homosexuality was not all that difficult to accept. I had camping trips, heavy metal concerts, and outings to Detroit to remind me of who my brother *really* was, not the public's chronicles of sexual deviance exercised in orgylike fashion in bathhouses and porn theaters. Besides, I had bigger demons than my own personal struggle to accept my brother's sexuality: others' homophobia. I worried about what my co-workers, friends, and other acquaintances would say or do.

The next morning, self-doubt plagued me. Did people know I was the brother of a gay man? Was it written all over my face? Would I be accepted at work, among the cereal-box toys and puffed-rice politics? I struggled to find answers.

Dressed in factory-mandated, pin-striped overalls, all my co-workers were gathered in the break room before the day started. I listened to their conversation and watched their body language. My brother's confession of the night before made me hypersensitive. I waited for the inevitable. How long would it take them to reveal what they must already know? Did Max, with his sweat-soaked bandanna and skeptical eye squint, know? Did Mary, the beautiful blonde with a runner's body, have any idea? It took several minutes to reassure myself that the fact of my brother's sexuality hadn't been published in the *Battle Creek Herald*. I relaxed enough to be able to sit with Max, Kevin, and Mary, listening to how Max had purposely poured beer on a football player's head.

"I would have," Max said, scratching his bandanna.

"You would have what?" Kevin said.

"I would have," continued Max.

"Right," Kevin chuckled. "You would have slapped the quarterback."

"Bitch-slapped him," insisted Max.

"Miller lost the fucking game for the team." Max was angry.

"So you decided to pour beer on his head?" Kevin asked in disbelief.

"I was two feet from the goal line," bragged Max. "There I was, beer in my hand, and him going to the locker room with his helmet off and dopey head hanging out in the open."

"Look who's talking," Mary piped in.

Max just looked at her quizzically (one trait Mary had was her ability to insult men without eliciting retaliation) and then continued: "I looked: beer in hand, helmet off, beer in hand, helmet off." Max held an imaginary cup, then looked away.

"And you did every simian in the stadium justice," Mary concluded.

"I tossed a beer all over his head," Max announced proudly.

"And you would have bitch-slapped him." Kevin said.

"If I coulda reached," Max insisted.

"You're such a humanitarian," Kevin said sarcastically.

"He's a fag! I had money on that game," Max said vindictively.

As Max let the word *fag* slip, I knew one thing: I wanted to do more than "bitch-slap" him. Even scarier was realizing I was now an outsider, and every peer I had once considered influential was against me, or might be in due time. People such as Max call others "fags" as if they were the worst form of humanity. If Max accidentally dropped a cereal box on the floor, others would quickly scold him, saying, "Pick it up, fag!" If they went to a bad movie or thought a musical group was inadequate they would describe it simply by saying, "That was gay."

"Son of a bitch shouldn't have lost the damn football game," Max concluded and looked at me like I was plotting to kill him. "What's up with you, Tom? You don't like that story? You got a bug up your ass?"

I sat there, looking at Max hoping he would excuse himself.

"Why was this guy a fag?" I said.

"He was a loser."

I felt like loosening his teeth. In a sense, he was saying my brother was a loser for simply choosing to be sexual.

"The fag lost the entire game." Max tried to defend his argument.

I was about to tell him the many ways I could shut his mouth permanently when Mary spoke for me.

"I feel like I'm in prison." Mary and I were both exasperated.

"Only eight more hours till the day's over," Max said to her.

"Yeah, but you'll be here tomorrow," she reminded us.

I dragged myself through the day, thinking that people such as Max would forever discriminate against my brother and me. I include myself because when my brother came out, I, by default, did too, not because I lusted after muscular thighs and buttocks, but because we were family. Dan's struggles were *my* struggles.

After work, I didn't go home right away. I sat in my car feeling an intense hatred for Max. Sure, he wasn't aware that my brother came out the night before; sure, he constantly made jokes about minorities; sure, when he made jokes about homos and dykes, he meant only to satirize humanity. He wasn't selective in his bigotry. When he referred to homosexual men, or even to his friends as "fags," however, he was perpetuating discrimination. In my mind, he became a straight man who could easily make the leap to brutal attacks on gay men. Max was dangerous. I sat in my car believing I needed to be the avenger of this hatred. All I had to do to stop it, I thought, was to stop Max. This would confirm that homophobia does not pay.

When I returned home that evening, dinnertime was a little quieter than usual, our first meal together since finding out that my brother was gay. My mother tried to converse, suggesting how the medical community could benefit from having more strong women nurses such as herself and the other gals at work. My dad just looked at his food, and when I spoke, he looked at me as if I, too, might come out one day. On the other side of the table, my brother was grinning uncomfortably. He spoke; I answered.

"Went to the movies today," Dan began.

"Which one?" I asked.

"Some movie about these little kids who were detectives and had to solve a bake sale murder."

"Isn't that a kids' movie?"

"Not really."

"Was it good?"

"Pretty good, except there were too many kids who kept laughing at the stupidest jokes."

"You liked it?

"Yeah."

"You going to start wearing cardigans and join a children's show on public television?" I ribbed.

We avoided what was really on our minds.

After dinner, Dan and I went upstairs while our parents did the dishes. I pulled out a hunter's knife from my pocket and placed it on my dresser. On my drive home from work, I had planned and plotted Max's demise. The Boy Scout knife, so useful in whittling that wooden derby car in grade school, would be useful again, this time to slash Max's tires.

"I might lose my job tomorrow," I confessed.

"What'd you do?" asked Dan.

"It's not what I did. It's what I'm going to do."

"What?"

"Max is a jerk."

"So?"

"So, I'm going to slash the tires of his car. He's a homophobic reject."

"Why?"

"He was saying some stuff today about you—about gay people."

"What'd he say?"

"He said this and that was gay. He called someone a fag."

"So?"

"He was saying stuff about you. He said the words *fag* and *gay*. That's why I want to slash his tires."

"Did he say, 'Danny's a fag'?"

"No. Well, practically."

"You're gonna lose your job because of that?"

"Well, they might trace it back to me if I—"

"Don't be stupid."

I was shocked that my brother didn't understand my reasoning and that he was chastising me.

"You know, if I slash his tires, it'll teach him a lesson."

"What lesson? To call *you* a fag, too? You're not going to teach Max anything."

His argument was convincing. I wanted to teach Max a lesson, but what lesson exactly? A lesson worth losing my job over?

"Dude," my brother said in his most serious "dude" tone. "You think that's the only way to stop homophobes?"

"I just wanted to—"

"You wanted to protect me. Protect yourself, man. What would Mom and Dad think? Just forget about it."

I felt as if I had given my brother a present and he wanted the receipt to take it back.

"You don't have to be a hero, you know. Max is already a loser. Don't mess up your life for his stupidity."

As much as I didn't want to admit it, Dan was right. I still thought about going out that night and was ready at a moment's notice to jump out of bed at 3 a.m. to go tire slashing. My brother, however, didn't want revenge, a fact I didn't fully understand or appreciate then.

One night about a year later, after I had moved out of the house to go to college, I was playing cards with some friends.

"Read 'em and weep, fags," my roommate said as he laid down his hand.

"You know, you sound ignorant when you say that."

"Say what—'Read 'em and weep'?"

"No—*fags*. You sound homophobic."

"Who am I offending?"

"Me."

"Why?"

"Because my brother's gay," I said with pride, minus the desire for revenge.

When Dan stopped me from slashing Max's tires that night five years ago, I was unknowingly learning how to deal with discrimination in another way. Instead of seeking to retaliate, I now try to educate the people around me. Dan taught me that I can't change people through violence, but I can tell others what I think and let them know I love and support my brother, a lesson I have learned well. Preserving my relationship with Dan and my family is the most important thing—always was, always will be.

8

More Than Family

Shari Hanofee

My brother, Wayne, was born fifteen years before I was. He is
fifty-two and I am thirty-seven. Sal, his partner of thirty years,
came into my life when I was seven years old, so he seems like a
brother to me in many ways too. Both Wayne and Sal have taught
me about love, acceptance, and the meaning of being true to myself.

Being the little sister, the baby, I was always surrounded with
lots of love. Wayne and Sal have been constants in my life, my role
models. My sister, Ellen, and her husband, Bill, also together for
thirty years, and also role models in their own ways, along with my
husband, my two children, and my three nieces, all make up my
circle of love.

My mom died ten years ago. At that point, I thought my circle
was shrinking, but it wasn't. It was getting stronger. The lessons of
unconditional love she taught continue to give us the strength to
carry on. She was the center of our family, the center of our world.
My mother always accepted all of her children as they were. She
was proud of us no matter what, and that sense of acceptance was
probably one reason I never wondered about my brother's sexuality. Because Wayne was much older, I didn't know him as a teenager. I never thought it was unusual that he and Sal lived together
or that they relocated to other states together. Sal was his roommate. No one told me differently or voiced objections. This was
life as I knew it. Wayne and Sal together—always.

My dad died when I was eight years old. Wayne moved back home after that and became the man of the house. The pain of losing my dad has overshadowed and blocked many of my early childhood memories, but having a brother who was on my side and whom I could respect helped. There was always a sense of safety when Wayne was around. I couldn't explain the dynamic between him and me back then, nor do I completely understand it now. My mom definitely was the parent. Wayne had a different role. His opinion meant a great deal to me, and I tried hard to please him. He made me laugh, taught me how to dance the hustle, and sometimes would take me to work with him.

I remember when he was a bank manager. His respect for others always set an example. The tellers, most of whom were women, loved him. I remember a conversation he had with one of them, when she had to go home because her menstrual cramps were unbearable. He never minimized the pain but allowed her to cope with the situation in her own way. Remembering that incident helped me to take my own body seriously. Wayne was the person who taught me how a woman should be treated and how I should treat myself. I am now an empowerment coach, helping other women learn how to take control of their bodies and their lives. I think my training started that day.

After Wayne moved out to live with Sal, they came to dinner weekly. We always laughed and had a great time. One of our most memorable meals was when I was about ten years old. I made the mistake of putting my finger—full of whipped cream—onto my brother's nose. He told me that, one day, I would be sorry I had done that. I just figured he would tease me or tickle me. It was worth it, I thought. About a month later during dinner, Wayne gave me the keys to his car and asked me to get something out of the trunk. I ran outside and happily returned with the bag in tow. As I opened the front door—*SMASH*—a whole pie plate full of whipped cream, right in my face! Oh, my big brother. We still laugh about that one.

It wasn't until I was a sophomore in high school, a naive fourteen-year-old, that I learned my brother was gay. I was probably one of the last in my family to know. It was the late 1970s. At the time, my mom and I lived outside New York City. We had moved there two years earlier. I was getting a dress out of my closet to show Wayne and Sal because I wanted their opinion about whether I should wear it to the party I was planning to attend. Pointing to another, I said to Wayne, "This is the dress I am going to wear at your wedding." Oblivious, I went on about the party, or something else perhaps, unaware of the look I am sure Wayne and Sal shared with Mom.

The next week, my brother asked me if I would go for a walk with him. He wanted to tell me something. When he said he was gay, I remember feeling a queasy sensation in my stomach. *Gay* had always been something bad, something that the guys at school teased one another about. How could my brother be gay? I was confused. After a couple of days of processing this new information and dealing with my own feelings about it, the idea of Wayne and Sal made sense. They loved each other. They were a family.

During the rest of my adolescence, I never told my friends about my brother, but I did not deny who he was, nor did I exclude Wayne and Sal from any conversation or event. Saying the words "My brother is gay," however, was difficult because of the stigma attached to homosexuality. My peers all seemed to have a preconceived notion of what being gay was: being bad, a sinner, a freak. I wanted my friends to meet Wayne and Sal *before* I told them they were gay, so that those stereotypes would be challenged. By the time I was in my twenties and more secure emotionally, I began telling everyone, when appropriate, and Sal and Wayne began to change my friends' perceptions of what *gay* truly means. They would say to me that Wayne and Sal were "so normal." I would answer, "You don't know my brother very well then!"

Although I never considered Wayne to be a father figure, he was the most influential man in my life while I was growing up. It only made sense to have him accompany me down the aisle on my wedding day. His written sentiments on my card expressed this:

> I am proud that our relationship has been so varied—brother and sister, parent and child, friends. I love you very much and this love allows us to get closer. I am proud and thankful that you have asked me to escort you down the aisle as you get married. To share that special moment in this special way

touches me deeply and allows my love for you to be seen by all.

A special period in our lives was when all of us became parents for the first time. Wayne and Sal adopted their daughter, Hope, one month before the birth of my first child, Shane. Dealing with the trials and tribulations of parenting has created a special bond, one I never imagined we would share together. In the hospital, the day my son was born, we told the nurses that Wayne and Sal were the grandfathers so they could stay longer to ogle their new nephew. We also told them that I had adopted Hope so she could be with us too—a white lie—but it was important to have them all with me on that eventful day.

Many years later, I was honored to attend Wayne and Sal's commitment ceremony. (No, I didn't wear that dress I showed Wayne so many years before.) I remember the phone call when he very excitedly told me he had asked Sal to marry him. At first I was a little confused. After twenty-eight years of living together, didn't they consider themselves already married? Wayne, however, wanted the ceremony, the public acknowledgment that they were more than just a couple. They wanted their union blessed and so it was off to Vermont, where gay unions are legal.

The drive there with my cousin and my daughter, on a gorgeous fall day, couldn't have been more glorious. The trees blazed with color, the excitement of the day building by the hour. We got to the inn where the ceremony was to be held. Wayne, Sal, and Hope; their friends, Betty and Margaret; and their son, Anthony, who was to be the best man, were already dressed. Milling around, finishing the final touches before we walked to the area where the ceremony would take place, my first thought was, "They are so happy." I gave my brother our mother's wedding ring, which she had given to me before she died. Mom was definitely shining down on us that day.

Wayne and Sal wanted an intimate ceremony, so not many people were invited, and some of them couldn't make it. Those who were there and those who weren't all blessed their union. It was not just this day—one full of joy, meaning, and love—that joined all of us to them and them to each other. It is also the support we give day to day, during the ups and downs, that matters most. This is what makes them, and all of us, a family.

We have always talked openly with our children, Shane and Alyssa, about their uncles' sexuality. When they were younger, we told them that when two people of the same sex love each other, that means they are gay, a word they both have heard their whole lives. My children love Wayne and Sal and know, in turn, that they are loved by them. That didn't mean, however, that every child they knew felt the same way they did about gay people.

My daughter, Alyssa, then age seven, came home from school upset one day. After telling some other students her uncle was gay, she was teased about it. I explained that not everyone is raised to be accepting of others who are different, that children are only as accepting as their parents are, and that their parents probably don't have anyone they love who is gay. Conversations about acceptance, what family means, AIDS, and loving others have all stemmed from discussions we have had about Uncle Wayne and Uncle Sal. Now that Shane and Alyssa are both teenagers, we discuss their difficulties with peer pressure, questions about their own identities, and questions about how our family has handled their Uncle Wayne being gay.

From what I have heard, my dad wasn't so enthralled with having a gay son—at first. Although he had met Sal only a few times before he died, my dad eventually considered him a "son-in-law." My sister, Ellen, had suspected that Wayne was gay when they were teenagers. "That was who Wayne was," was how she thought about it. I don't know if most of us were just accepting, if we were in denial, or if Wayne, being the loving person he is, set the tone for the rest of us.

There are so many facets to my complex, ever-evolving relationship with Wayne. We are not just family; we are friends and confidants. We laugh together, cry together, bitch together, and share our lives together. My brother's sexuality affected me in only one way: It helped me always to be proud of who I am, to hold my head up high, and to be true to myself.

9

A Road Less Traveled

Lisa B. Lewis

Henry and I grew up in what is commonly known as a dysfunctional family. Mom and Dad probably never should have married in the first place. Their very different worldviews made them ill suited for each other. Sometimes, however, good can come from bad. Henry and I were definitely the best things that came out of that relationship.

There was never any peace in our home. Our parents argued constantly and would frequently keep both of us up at night. I remember getting my brother out of bed, putting on our most pitiful faces, going upstairs, and pleading, "Mommy and Daddy, will you please keep it down so we can sleep?" I'm not sure what effect we hoped for, but there we were—a team.

Since our parents fought, my brother and I, imitating what we saw, fought too, particularly when someone was around to notice. Alone, with no one paying any attention, we got along just fine.

Siblings can react differently to their circumstances. I always needed to be the boss, because, reflecting back on that time, I obviously had no real control of my world. My brother, in contrast, became intensely shy. I told Henry whatever I thought he wanted to hear so I could get my way: "You can have twenty games all *your* way if I get this one *my* way." He always gave in. (I still owe him those twenty games many times over.) Once, I decided his favorite color had to be yellow so it would match my favorite color at the time—red. Certainly life could not continue if our favorite colors did not match. As an adult, I look back and regret how manipulative I was. Henry forgave me long before I ever forgave myself.

The year 1974 was a turning point for us. My parents divorced. I was six years old; my brother was four years old. We were living in Memphis, Tennessee. Our lives seemed fairly normal to us—schoolwork, playing games, family events. Although Mom did her best, things were difficult for women in those days. They were usually paid less for doing more work than men did, and good jobs were hard to come by. I remember a talk she had with us. She said, "We're going to have to cut back. We have only seven dollars left in our checking account." I asked, "Does that mean I can't have twenty-five cents for candy?" Mom reassured me she would dig deep to find it in a "candy emergency."

I think her difficulties getting work in Memphis, along with the stigma of the divorce, contributed a great deal to Mom's decision to give us all a fresh start. So when I was eleven and Henry was nine, we moved from Memphis to Atlanta. This was a major change for all of us. Not only had my brother and I grown up in Tennessee, but my mother and her parents had as well. We were a close-knit group—Mom, Henry, and I. Mom found ways to make it all fun—turning life's lemons into lemondae. We looked on this move as a grand adventure.

After the move, Mom felt more fulfilled professionally than she ever had and Henry and I got a new start. Mom had to work eighty hours a week as a college professor, so given that we didn't know anyone else in town at first, my brother and I bonded even more. At least we had each other. New kids rarely make the most-popular list and we were both teased incessantly by our peers. Although I could take it and fought back hard, Henry couldn't. I got into several fights trying to defend him.

After three years in Atlanta, we moved to Athens, Georgia, so Mom could fulfill the one-year residency requirement needed to complete her PhD in theater history. Then it was on to Lexington, Kentucky, where she taught at the university for two years. All three moves—Atlanta, Athens, and Lexington—were easier for me than for Henry, who had more difficulty making friends than I did. Being the new kid and having to wear thick, brown-rimmed glasses made him an easy victim.

After two years in Kentucky, my mother got another job in Beloit, Wisconsin. This time the two of them went without me. It was time to strike out on my own. Henry seemed to thrive: he made some friends, finished high school, and then went to college there. Perhaps my absence helped him. I often thought he spent too much time in my shadow.

As adults, Henry and I are about as different as two people can be. I am very outgoing and have my own family entertainment business. For me, every day is different. My brother earned a master's degree in business administration and loves working in an office with a regular schedule, a boss, and benefits. We share a deep love and respect for each other, and he is one of the dearest people in the world to me.

At age thirty-one, three years ago, when Henry called to tell me he was gay, it was no great surprise. According to him, my exact words were, "Don't rush into anything." He responded that he was not rushing, considering the fantasies he had had since puberty. I responded with, "In that case, you have to meet my friend Doug."

Mom responded similarly. She always had many gay friends and figured Henry would fit in just fine. Her only regret was that he hadn't come out earlier in life so that she could have fixed him up with someone. His friends didn't seem to care, and although some seemed surprised, they are all still his friends.

For Henry it was difficult, especially at first. I hurt for him because *he* was hurting. He wanted those things in life commonly associated with being straight—a spouse and kids. The gay road is one less traveled, and so it can be, and frequently is, rockier. Once completely out, though, he became a new man. He made new friends, joined a new social circle, and started a relationship—one that didn't last that long, but a better one than he had ever had with a female. I am thrilled that he has started on a path to peace and happiness. Living as if he were someone he was not tore him up inside. He is much happier now.

Henry's being gay has always been a nonissue for me. Each day Henry must see his own reflection in the mirror, and he alone must be comfortable with the man staring back at him.

I think Henry strongly felt the lack of our father's presence while growing up. At sixty years old, Dad decided he wanted a closer relationship with his biological children. My brother's coming out was a challenge for the two of them. A gay son is still not the norm in the small conservative community in which my father lives, but both of them seem to be working hard to overcome all the bumps in that road.

My own relationship with my brother has been very close throughout our lives. Nothing is different now except, instead of asking him about girlfriends, I ask him about boyfriends, hoping that the person he dates is good to him and makes him happy.

We should look at who people are inside—their soul—not their skin color, the shape of their bodies, or with whom they share their bed. My brother has one of the kindest, most compassionate hearts in the world. I will keep hoping that he finds the one special person who will treasure him and love him for the rest of his life. He deserves no less and much more.

– 10 –

Step-by-Step

Luke Markert

When someone asks if I have any siblings, I always hesitate—slightly. It's complicated because my brother lives overseas with his partner, whom he met while attending college. That leads to other questions, such as, "Oh, is he in the military?" If I'm talking with someone I don't know very well or detect a whiff of Christian conservatism, I give the safe, nonconfrontational answer: "He just finished college and is living abroad with a friend for a while until he goes to graduate school."

John, now twenty-five years old, is a great guy—funny, smart, and an extremely talented musician. He graduated from high school near the top of his class and was an honor student at the University of Houston, graduating with a degree in organ performance. Because I was six years older, John and I were never that close growing up. We never developed that tight bond that some brothers do. Our age difference was not the only reason for that. John *was* different: he never had a girlfriend in high school; he never took an interest in sports; he preferred helping Mom in the kitchen rather than helping Dad mow the lawn; and his passion was music.

John came out to us when he was a senior in high school. I will never forget the afternoon we all gathered around the dinner table. John had told my parents first, so Dad brought the four of us together to make sure I was aware of the situation too. As the conversation unfolded, I remember experiencing a sense of disbelief and shock. It was almost as if I had been deceived. Surely this couldn't be! "We've got to do something about this!" I said desperately to my parents. John had obviously struggled to keep his sexuality a secret and had not always been honest—something that was not tolerated in our family. My dad, however, was calm and caring. He just asked John to be open with us. Looking back, I truly appreciate the compassion and love my dad showed toward John during that difficult time.

I was about twenty-three then and had been out of college for a year. The acceptance my parents displayed was as much of a shock to me as finding out John was gay. Our family is of German descent with strong ties to the Lutheran Church. To make matters more complicated, we were Missouri Synod Lutheran, which was, and continues to be, one of the more fundamental conservative divisions within the Lutheran Church. Distinct differences exist between Missouri Synod Lutherans and the more progressive Evangelical Lutherans, whom we eventually joined. The chasm that separates these two factions is so deep they almost appear to be distinct religious denominations.

My conservative upbringing contributed to the notion that John's behavior was sinful. The first thought I had about it was that my brother had somehow been misdirected, involving himself in the wrong crowd. How could he be gay? I was convinced we all had to help him overcome this problem. I equated being gay with having a mental disorder and thought maybe we should send him to a therapist.

I was certain my parents would be angry, sad, or both. My dad, the disciplinarian, was the one we always had to answer to. I love, admire, and respect my father, but I was sure he would be outraged. Mom, always the compassionate one, played the mediator when there was a disagreement between my dad and me. Surely she would have to assume this role to keep the peace in the family. Much to my surprise, Dad stood up for John. Mom later confided in me that she had been heartbroken when she found out. Her hopes and dreams of both boys marrying and giving her grandchildren had been dashed. She has since overcome her disappointment, but it was difficult at first. Turning to the church for guidance led to my parents being ousted for not condemning my brother's "sinful lifestyle," a consequence they had not expected.

That's when we joined the Evangelical Lutheran Church across town. The congregation accepted John with open arms and, shortly thereafter, he became one of the organists.

My parents' quest to understand continued as they read books and talked to others. They came to the conclusion that being gay is not a choice, but rather a predetermined biological variance. My dad explained to me that homosexuality was a sort of "cruel trick Mother Nature plays." That may have been an oversimplification but, at the time, it was very effective. As a child growing up in the 1980s, I made a distinct association between the spread of HIV/AIDS and the "homosexual lifestyle." It didn't take much to convince me that God was punishing gays. My dad's explanation allowed me to take that first small step toward both accepting my brother and changing my perspective on homosexuality.

My mom related many sad accounts of gay teenagers being kicked out of their homes after coming out to their parents. Even worse were the stories of suicides, resulting from depression and rejection. My mother and father definitely deserved a Parents of the Year Award in 1995. Not only did they accept my brother with open arms, but they also established a PFLAG (Parents, Families and Friends of Lesbians and Gays) chapter in our hometown and developed positive relationships with other successful, well-educated gay people in our community as well as in Houston, where my brother later attended college. That was an eye-opener for me—another important step in deconstructing my own stereotypes. At that time, I didn't perceive gays and lesbians as being affluent, upper-middle-class people. Most of them, however, didn't look or act "gay." Now I am more open-minded, I am more tolerant of those who are different, and I try to look beneath the surface and not let first impressions get in my way.

A couple of years after John's disclosure, while I was living and working in Connecticut, my parents and John came to visit. By this time, they were all involved in PFLAG, lobbying Congress for passage of the Employment Non-Discrimination Act. Their visit coincided with National Gay Pride Month. Because of our proximity to New York City, they insisted on attending the Gay Pride Parade there. Although I was more accepting of John than I had been, at the time I was still a little uncomfortable being "in his element." I was making progress, though, and that parade proved to be a turning point, yet another step in my journey toward acceptance.

I will never forget how, as we marched down Fifth Avenue, the people cheered and waved at us. I wasn't quite sure what all the commotion was about or even what the significance of the march was—until later that day. As the pace slowed, we stopped to talk with others. One young man, who said it was nice to see us marching as a family, went on to tell us how his own family had disowned him after he came out. That moment, for me, was an epiphany. I finally understood what acceptance was all about. How many hundreds or thousands of people lining the streets that day had similar stories to tell? How many of them grew up in the absence of tolerant and loving parents such as mine?

PART II:
ON HAVING A LESBIAN SISTER

11

Sara and I

Kate Boesser

I'm lying in bed, age four, covered with only a sheet. Next to me lies Sara, only a year older, but infinitely wiser. On the dresser sits the fan, turning slowly to her side, then to mine, then back to hers. Sweat pours off our bodies. We can't sleep. She's telling me about her make-believe watch that she insists tells time. I want her to show me how it works. We sneak over to the door, crack it, look down the hall, and observe our parents having a party several feet away. We cross the hall, enter the bathroom, then turn on the light. Sara delights me with instructions about the watch. We sneak back across the hall and into our own room. A few minutes later, I want to see it again. We head for the bathroom. We go over and back several more times, until Dad looks in on us. By then, Sara is safely back in the bedroom, but I'm not. He grabs me and spanks me just once, and I cry and cry. Sara feels bad because it was her watch and I got punished. She tells me she's sorry.

I think Sara wants to be alone, but it's always "Sara, Kate, and the little girls" (our two younger sisters, less than a year apart). So it's Sara and I—always. Sara begrudgingly leads the way on her bike, me on my tricycle, down the dirt road and over the bridge. We watch cowboys and cowgirls circling barrels on horses in a field nearby. Now it's time to go home. We get to the bridge, and I'm tired. I can't keep up with her. She's crossed over first, and then I come up onto the bridge. There in the middle is a large snake. I can't get across. I call to her, but her patience with me is shot. She tells me not to be a chicken, to come on across. I can't. I beg her to wait, to come back and ride with me. She refuses and rides ahead. I scream, have to wait for what seems like forever, but finally make it across.

Our dad takes us both fishing—first Sara, then me—before we catch the school bus. We go out on the lake, eat cereal from the box, dangle lines in the water. It's a special time with Dad. I've been throwing tantrums lately, so he has been taking only Sara along. But I feel better one night, so Dad tells me he'll take me in the morning. Sara senses it's important for me to go and encourages me to turn all my clothes inside out so I'll wake up and laugh and be in a good mood and be ready. I wake up really angry instead, and no amount of laughter or encouragement from Sara helps. She gets to go fishing, and I stay home—again.

Sara is a tomboy. Her first sentence is "Fro me de ball." A photo is taken of her standing in North Carolina or Texas—I can't remember where. She is shirtless, catching a ball. She rides a bike, rides a horse, helps us catch tadpoles, and sets up containers to raise them in. She hangs onto the rope attached to the back of the car seat, pretending she's a cowgirl, riding wildly along as the car moves down the road. She doesn't scream when Dad uses the hoe to chop up snakes curled up on the hot driveway when we come home in the car. Being the oldest, she is given more responsibility than the rest of us.

We've moved to Juneau, Alaska—an incredible place. Sara is seven, I am six, and our sisters are five and four. We live in a fantastic house built in the 1800s, once the mansion of the territorial governor. Now it is the rectory, and it sits across the street from the church our dad runs. The image of it lingers. On its narrow cement steps stand we four girls—tallest to smallest—each dressed in starched dresses, white gloves, Easter hats, and new catalog black patent leather shoes.

Up the many steps sits a glassed-in porch, a large many-paned window through which Sara once shoved me. It is Sunday morning, and I am screaming and dripping blood from my wrist. Dad comes back from church dressed in his white robes, gathers me up, then walks the two blocks up the hill to the hospital where I get stitches. Sara is pretty kind to me for a while after this. But I have to watch out. She's pretty tough.

Upstairs in the unheated attic is where Sara and I sleep. In Sara's slope-roofed room there is a window with the fire escape knotted rope hanging to the ground outside. Next to her bed is a latch holding two doors shut, opening onto the ceiling joists above the living room. Antiques cover the dusty timbers: a broken once-beautiful chandelier; pots and pans; vases; trunks full of old clothes; glass eyes; and shoes. My room is on the other side of these treasures. Through the walls at night Sara and I sing and tap messages, and I often go to sleep to the tunes of her small oval decorated music box—another attic find. Sara raises and trains mice and stores bags of white bread and red licorice for her snacks. She also has a wind-up gramophone and some old records.

Sara plays ball. She's the only girl included in all of the neighborhood teams. Even the tough Catholic schoolboys want her because she's really good. My sister, this brown-haired, long-braided tomboy, is "best player" on the block. Once she hits a ball and breaks a neighbor's window. It's pretty serious, so our parents talk to her about going next door and telling them it was her fault. She then saves her money and pays them back.

We play a game called "guess the time and temperature," racing on our bikes along the sidewalks to view a large lit sign showing both. The one who guesses closest is the winner. Who do you think always wins?

We roller-skate on the rough sidewalks, knees covered with Band-Aids. We watch out for each other, then scream down San Francisco–like hills past many cross streets, all the way down Gold till it turns into Gastineau. In winter we go up where the steepest street is blocked off and sled down. We also go skiing. Sara, bless her heart, carries my skis up the mountain weekend after weekend. She sticks with me as I learn to ski, helping me on the rope tow. We come down the mountain together when each cold wet day is over. We walk without gear across the bridge and each buy a donut at the bakery, dripping and shivering while waiting for Mom to come pick us up.

Sara has Friends—with a capital *F.* I don't. I make friends—with a small *f*—get mad at them, pit them against one another, pass on rumors, make fun of them, then buddy-buddy up with them. All my friends do this too, but not Sara. Her Friend is someone special, one with whom you are always honest, one you treat as gold. It's rare and real, and I often marvel at her. She tries to explain it to me, but I don't get it.

From our small rowboat we go fishing, spending all day at Lena Cove pulling in a Dolly Varden trout here and there, but mostly bullheads. Sara always agrees to gut and clean the fish. One day, though, we come ashore and she says, "Okay, Kate, that's it. From now on you clean your own fish." She leaves me there frustrated and begging. She knows we can't bring them into the house until they're cleaned and ready to cook, and it's a waste to throw them back in the water once we've killed them. I stand there and stare at that ugly fish and tell myself that if Sara can do it, so can I. Finally, I cut into its gut, slice it up, and remove its innards. It isn't so hard after all, I think, and I feel proud when I show Sara the cleaned fish as I bring it into the house.

We're teenagers now, the four Boesser girls, first in junior high, then high school, all at the same time. Our old home has been torn down, and we're now living in a boring box of a modern house. Sara and I have rooms next to each other. She paints her room white with green-trimmed curtains. I paint mine pink, add pink-and-white eyelet bedding, and curtains. Sara has good taste in clothes—traditional and plain but nice. She wears plaid pleated wool skirts and matching knee socks and sweaters or blouses, while I make my own clothes from Simplicity and McCall's patterns. Every morning Sara asks me a million times how she looks: Does this skirt match this blouse? Is it the right length? It bugs me because I always think she looks good in her short hair and matching outfits.

Sara plays for GAA: Girls' Athletic Association. She travels to Canada, and we watch her compete. She's a point guard, a point maker, even a three-pointer at times, so I'm really proud of her. But I'm starting to get interested in watching the guys play high school basketball.

A boy, a family friend, has invited Sara out to a movie. She doesn't want to go, and I don't understand why. He seems harmless and nice enough, and he really likes her. It seems like no big deal, but she refuses. So I say I'll go with him instead. When he comes to the house, he's disappointed, but he agrees to go with me anyway. He spends the whole boring time telling me how much he likes Sara and how she won't give him the time of day; I tell him details about her and assure him maybe she'll change her mind. She never does.

I'm on drill team. Our coach is also the physical education teacher and the GAA coach. She's a big tough woman, whom I don't like very much, but Sara thinks the world of her. The coach hits us on the ankles with a yardstick for not picking up our feet high enough, which I think is ridiculous. She seems really bossy and kind of a mean character. One morning at practice, I overhear my friends talking about how the coach invited some girls to her house and recommended a racy movie. The drill team alludes that these are girls who like feeling and kissing one another. I block out the words. Sara goes to the coach's house and then to the movies. My parents know about it, but it's no big deal to them. Could my friends be suggesting that Sara is weird?

I start to think of Sara as different—not considering the possibility that she likes other girls, just that she enjoys their company. Those relationships are far more important for her than for me. I also start to be protective, just a bit. I observe her relationships with everybody.

Here comes another one: a truly nice guy, a gymnast. They are just buddies. Then an older man, who is "head over heels" for Sara, comes along. He will not give up, talks to my mom about Sara, remaining steadfastly determined. Sara remains distant. Then, after she graduates high school, there is an older teacher. She turns him down right from the start. Can't they all see she's not interested?

By now, Sara is an incredible tennis player, challenging the older businessmen, other avid tennis players who are Dad's age and members of the Rotary Club. I don't know any of them. She and I go to Anchorage to see Arthur Ashe play. Incredible! We also go skiing at Alyeska, and bomb down the hill all day long. I join the cross-country ski team. It's the only sport I think I can possibly excel at, though I'll never be as good as Sara. I really don't want to compete with her, not at sports anyway. I do have to compete with my younger sisters for boyfriends; we literally seem to fall in love with the same guys. This never happens between Sara and me.

We have a bond; we tell each other our dreams; we notice synchronicities. I think we appreciate each other. One day, Sara says she's not going to church anymore—just like that. I didn't know it was an option. I can't believe her guts. Mom and Dad say it's her decision. Wow!

Sara goes off to college in California, and I get to visit her. She has a room to herself since her roommate has moved out. It's a high-class college, but I don't think Sara's so keen on it. In fact, she moves to Oregon, and then Washington to finish school. Each time, I visit her. We ride horses together down under a freeway during a flash flood with the ground turning to slick mud, and we can't get the horses out of the ditch for miles. We come back drenched. Another time we throw a pineapple and a coconut out of her third-story window to crack them open, then run downstairs to pick up the pieces.

I go to college clear across the country from Sara. We call and talk for hours. Music of the early 1970s impresses us. We hold the phone next to the stereo to play the latest songs to each other. Sara gets a past-life reading and calls to tell me about it, has been in a peace march, and smashes her truck. I've marched too, been in cross-country ski races, and learned about life.

Sara takes a break from college and is living in a cold house with roommates. I visit and wish better for her; wish her friends wouldn't belittle her; wish they'd treat her with greater respect; wish they'd notice how strong and honest and true she is. I guess I know she's gay by now, though we don't talk about it. I don't call her and say, "Guess what? I think I've fallen in love with this guy." Neither does she call me and say, "Guess what? I think I've fallen in love with this woman." We've entered our sexual worlds in parallel places, and we both understand each other without the need to question. Her friends are young women, while mine since childhood have always included males *and* females. She is more a "women's libber," living in a woman's world, apart from mine. She encourages me to be more outspoken, to be strong, to notice other women around me.

Much later my sister asks me something: "Come on. Didn't you ever act on feelings for another woman? Doesn't it reside in everyone?" And I do admit I have loved someone and was upset when she married her girlfriend, and that, yes, I did have the chance to act on it, but it didn't work out. So I figure I'm pretty much heterosexual. I've come to believe, having raised two daughters who are total opposites and having taught many others, that sexuality is on a continuum. Attractions can be purely male, less male, less female, purely female. But Sara and I don't spend much time talking science.

Sara has been in Seattle for a while, and she has come out to our parents, which didn't surprise them, I don't think. She's moved something like twelve times in four years and is now part of a woman's cooperative, repairing houses. She drives me all over a section of town, pointing out the houses she's renovated, talking about the bathrooms she's remodeled. My partner and I help her clean up one of her repossessed houses from the city, which she then resells for a profit.

We go dancing together. I meet some fun-loving people, many of whom scare me. Sara is out there dancing with her partner and I am alone sipping a drink. A large, deep-voiced woman comes up behind me and says, "You look scared, honey." I hit that dance floor fast, madly stepping out next to Sara and her partner. Whew! Hold on!

I figure that when I spend time with Sara, I want to try to be reasonably comfortable in her environment. I have to show her I can have fun in the way she has fun; that some of these butch girls don't scare me; that the wild freeness of it all is absolutely acceptable. I wouldn't find myself here without her—for sure. Still, it is indeed pretty awesome, I feel stronger for being here, and I do have fun.

Sara quits the cooperative and moves back up north where we were raised, then a town of 6,000, now a town of 25,000. She's a bold, outspoken, political, progay advocate out there. She asks my parents to make themselves heard, which my dad wouldn't do if she didn't ask. My mom dives into each cause, always supportive. They both are. I speak out, too, and feel so proud of my sister: so calm, so beautiful, so unthreatening, always knowing she'll make a difference one tiny step at a time, in a world moving sluggishly to accept all people. Her face, her story, her words, and her letters to the editor are all over the newspapers. I'm so proud, as is my whole family. "My sister is a gay rights advocate," we say. The sign she carries and is photographed with at a Washington, DC, rally reads: "We are your family, your co-workers, your friends. You love us already." Yes! I join PFLAG: Parents, Families and Friends of Lesbians and Gays.

Sara's story is included in the book *Making History: The Struggle for Gay and Lesbian Equal Rights, 1945-1990* (Marcus, 1993), an anthology of personal histories of gays and lesbians. Her chapter is "The Brave Alaskan—Sara Boesser." Brave to come out in a small Alaskan town in which she grew up; brave to stand up and be counted so that others can do the same.

My husband and I are raising two girls. Sara is an incredible aunt, who tries to understand and support each of her nieces. She and her partner invite our sports-minded daughter to stay with them and go to baseball camp; sends them each games, books, and gift certificates; teaches them to drive in the city; and then trusts them with her car. They, in turn, love her and trust in her friendship.

I, too, find in her space a refuge. Unlike my child-filled life, hers seems uncluttered and focused, clean and ordered, quiet and peaceful, full of direction and purpose. And now that our parents have retired and moved back into town, she's watching out for them—something I admire and appreciate. When I get anxious or ill, she's there for me. I drop in on her too much; I break into her space. I expect it to be okay, since we've been each other's partners since lying in the Texas heat sharing the fan so many years ago. I need her. I'm not sure if she needs me.

In contrast to Sara, her partner of twenty-two years does not refer to herself as gay or lesbian, does not think of herself as part of any movement, and feels every human being is unique and should not be labeled. How she can live with an activist, whose home office space resembles a political campaign headquarters, surprises me. She maintains a sense of confidence, a silence, and a way of being unique, separate from Sara. Neither one is better. It's just amazing they match so well.

There's pain: Sara's thirties and forties are packed with advocacy struggles. Political moves to protect people against discrimination based on sexual orientation fail time and again. Sara feels personally assaulted. She struggles to put this into perspective, to see that each fight brings gay rights into the light, brings people out of the closet, brings friends and relatives out as well, and makes the world a better place. She gets anxious and steps out of the political arena for a while. I didn't expect she'd stay in it forever. Did *she?*

Now Sara is fifty years old, and soon I will be as well. She watches as younger gay people pen the newsletters and go off to marches. She still writes her share of editorials and has begun to collect articles on gay and lesbian issues, which she sends out on the Internet to hundreds of us eagerly awaiting news. Still a visible issue embracer, she has changed the world, and she intends to keep on doing so into the second half of her life.

By example, Sara continually encourages me to do the same in those arenas of my life needing exposure and voice. I expect to continue to rely on her, step into her life, because we've been and always will be an intimate part of each other's lives. I can't extricate myself from her.

I attend PFLAG meetings, testify in public against discrimination, attend workshops, write letters to the editor, and am warned by my boss to "watch who my friends are" while teaching in our small town. That's when I really get a taste of what Sara has had to deal with her whole life. I fight prejudice, not only because of my sister, but also because I care about the state of the world. I'd like to think I'd stand up for this cause even if I didn't have a sister who is a lesbian.

Knowing Sara has helped me in so many ways. As a teacher, I met a family who had just moved here from a large Southern town because their son was being ridiculed. They wanted to live in an atmosphere where he'd be safe and be appreciated for his uniqueness. I understood. I'm so glad I was there for them.

Since childhood, Sara and I have always had a special language. If something goes wrong, we've always asked each other to send white light. "My friend is really sick. Send white light." "You're going into surgery soon. I will send you white light." "I'm exhausted. Could you send white light?" I've come to realize Sara actually *is* white light. So am I.

How fortunate we are sisters.

REFERENCE

Marcus, E. (1993). The brave Alaskan—Sara Boesser. In *Making history: The struggle for gay and lesbian equal rights, 1945-1990* (pp. 464-473). New York: HarperPerennial.

12

Speak No Evil

Brad Randall

My sister Sara came out to our parents in 1992. Twenty-six years old then, now thirty-six, she believes they knew about her lesbianism several years before that. Wanting to leave no doubt in their minds, she wrote them a letter. They reacted predictably: shock, guilt, disappointment, then gradual acceptance. Our four older siblings—Pat, forty-six, John, forty-five, James, forty-four, and Donna, forty-one—all responded with varying degrees of confusion, anger, and love. As a self-absorbed, fourteen-year-old and the only child still living home then, the announcement was well off my radar. My own reaction wouldn't come until several years later. Now twenty-four years old, still the baby, my family tried to protect me from information they thought could have been harmful. No matter how much I believed myself to be a critical-thinking youth, I was naive about my sister's lesbianism for a very long time. But let's start from the beginning.

My family is from a small, very Southern town in the south-western part of Virginia. Racism was, and still is, a serious issue there. I can remember my dad telling me about prejudice when I was very young, and ever since then, I cringe when someone tells a racist joke. During my first few years of high school, a time when peer pressure and conforming is most important, I had several racist friends. I fought a kind of silent opposition to the racism I saw, refusing to laugh at jokes and comments, not quite sure enough of myself to speak out. As I got older and developed into a leader in my high school, I became more outspoken. Looking back, this co-incided with the gradual awareness that my sister might be gay.

Up to that point in my life, the words *fag* and *queer* were incredibly uncreative weapons in the arsenal of insults my close friends and I lobbed at one another. We never meant anything derogatory to gays and lesbians; we just wanted to put one another down. I can't recall a time when any of us ever picked on someone because we actually thought he or she might be gay or lesbian. Sure, there were some students who were considered gay, but no one really knew and no one really cared enough to find out.

Sometime during my junior year of high school, I realized the woman my sister had been living with for the past few years probably wasn't just a roommate. I began questioning and evaluating my beliefs: Did I really think homosexuality was wrong? Did women have to act in a certain way and men in another? If it was unacceptable to make racist jokes, was it acceptable to make gay jokes? As I mentioned earlier, I had never been impressed with some of my friends' racist ideas. Now I was slowly forcing myself to look at our collective homophobia. Although I still was not 100 percent sure of my sister's lesbianism, I realized it was time to change not only my vocabulary but also my outlook.

After high school, I went away to college and began dating a woman who attended a neighboring university. We all had the idea that her roommate was a lesbian, but she wasn't out when I first met her. During the first semester of my sophomore year, she disclosed to me, saying, "Do you know any gay people?" I said, "I'm not sure, but I think my sister might be a lesbian." Bluntly, she said, "Well, I'm a lesbian." I'll never forget the look of petrified anticipation on her face. She seemed so vulnerable—seeking acceptance, braced for rejection, smiling nervously the whole time. I told her it was no problem for me. That's when I decided I should probably ask my sister the big question. It took another few months to summon the courage.

The following spring, I was at Sara's house for a cookout. Her "housemate" Nicole asked me what I had done the night before. Finally, this was my chance, I thought. I told her I had gone with some friends to The Park, a gay club we frequented in Roanoke where we could get in without being twenty-one years old. The look of confusion on Nicole's face was almost comical: "Did you say The Park?" She had taken the bait. Now I just had to wait to see what would happen.

After most of my family had left, Nicole approached me. "Your sister wants to ask you something," she said with a grin. I walked around and found Sara sitting in a lawn chair. She looked at me nervously and inquired, "Nicole said you went to The Park last night. Do Mom and Dad know?" "No, they don't know," I said, laughing. After a few seconds of awkward silence, we talked about why I went there, how often I had been, and whether I felt weird going to a gay club. Then, very nervously, I looked at my sister and asked, "So, you, you and Nicole are, a, umm . . ." "Yes," she interrupted, saving me from butchering the question any more than I already had. One would think that with the amount of time I had had to consider it, I would have been a little less nervous. She asked if I was okay with it, and I said, "Of course." She seemed happy.

Honestly, I don't remember much about the other parts of the conversation. Asking that question overshadowed the rest of the afternoon. It was such a big deal because no one in my family had ever talked to me about sex, sexuality, or even relationships. Asking Sara felt to me as if I were breaking a family code. That's one reason she never came out to me, and because I was the youngest, the issue was even more taboo.

I remember my mom signing a permission slip for me to be in the sex education portion of health class in high school and saying, "Well, someone has to teach you about this." What she didn't know was that the older kids on the school bus had done the job, albeit an incomplete education, years earlier. My parents' influence helped me not to fall victim to the racism of our hometown, but no one in my family said anything—good or bad—about gays and lesbians. Although I believe my parents had pretty much come to terms with Sara's lesbianism, no one wanted to say the word *gay* because they were worried I might figure something out. Their avoidance, combined with my sex education classes never touching on anything related to homosexuality, and the media's depictions of gays and lesbians as either overly flamboyant or extremely butch, left no doubt in my mind why it took me so long to put two and two together.

My sister being a lesbian wasn't that big a deal then. I had time to consider my opinions before the actual disclosure—an option I don't think our older siblings had—so it wasn't *that* much of a shock. With the first challenge behind me came the next: letting others know I was "gay friendly." It was easy with my close friends. I had talked about it with some of them already, and, at that point, although most had grown out of their ultrahomophobic phase, I still sensed homophobia and heterosexism there. Although not blatant, everyone's vocabulary had yet to evolve alongside mine. My friends were supportive of both my sister and me. They couldn't have been cooler, actually. It was my newer friends who posed the real challenge.

I was in the middle of pledging a fraternity the fall semester of my junior year, and quite a few hypermasculine guys wanted to make it perfectly clear that they were not gay and didn't like gay people. One day, I decided I had heard enough. All of my pledge brothers were in a room and someone made a remark about the "faggot who cut his hair." I don't remember what I said, but I was close to tears. I said something akin to "Guys, I have something that's really been bothering me." I went on about how my sister was a lesbian, how some of their comments were really ignorant, how badly it hurt keeping this bottled up, and if they had a problem with it, I didn't want to be around them. Their reactions were mixed. Some never said anything; some told me later they had gay relatives and friends and were glad I had spoken up; some didn't agree with me but respected my beliefs and would try to consider what they said. I completed my pledge period hoping for the best. (Oddly enough, one of the older brothers whom I befriended, the most homophobic of the bunch, came out to me three years later.)

During my junior year, I took a social history class, followed by a course on the Vietnam War. Both turned me on to becoming more politically active. During my senior year, I enrolled in two sociology classes along with a course on twentieth-century history, all of which opened my eyes to the plight of minorities, including women and the gay, lesbian, bisexual, and transgender communities. I had found my niche. I told my advisor I wanted to go to graduate school for sociology rather than history, and that I intended to study gay and lesbian issues. A history professor herself, she was disappointed with my decision but understood. However, she alerted me that others might suspect I was gay if I pursued this. That didn't bother me. To worry would be childish. I saw this new direction both as a challenge to myself and as a way to break down barriers by encouraging others to think. So what if people thought I was gay. At least they would be thinking.

The next summer I moved to Richmond, Virginia, to begin graduate school. One of the first people I met was Glen. We worked together at a multicultural center where the topic of discrimination and gay rights arose frequently. There I was very open about my sister being a lesbian. After a few weeks, Glen told me he was gay, then invited me to join the Sexual Minority Student Alliance. The meetings were fun and I met several new people. The gay-straight climate in Richmond was much different from the ones in my hometown and at college. However, there would soon be a shocking reminder of antigay sentiment that would change my life.

On September 22, 2000, a man by the name of Ronald Gay stopped someone on a Roanoke street and asked where he could find a gay bar. The person pointed him in the direction of the Backstreet Café, a local gay-friendly establishment. A mentally unstable drifter, who despised his last name for the torment it brought him, Gay chose this night to vent his anger. Walking into the Backstreet Café, he opened fire, wounding six people, killing one. The news sent shock waves through me. My sister had gone there often, and my friends and I had been to another gay club in the same city many times. This tragic event didn't happen in some far away place. It happened less than forty-five miles from my hometown. At that moment, my sister's lesbianism became real to me. She could just as easily have been the victim.

In response, I wrote a long e-mail to my friends and family to impress upon them the importance of contacting their elected officials about taking a stand against hate crimes. Several people responded quickly, not understanding how such a thing could have occurred. Some said they had already contacted their representatives and senators. My parents even replied. They wanted to help.

Later that night, Mom and Dad called to tell me I should expect to hear from my brother John. Apparently, he was upset because I had sent the e-mail to his wife at work. Her boss could have seen it and held it against her. I hadn't sent it to their home e-mail address because I didn't have it. They said John was glad I hadn't because his two sons, my nephews, might have seen it. They went on to tell me that John had problems with Sara's partner, Nicole, attending family functions, as he was concerned about the influence it might have on their kids. Though Sara had told me earlier that John was uncomfortable with her sexual orientation, I never knew how bad it really was.

As expected, John called me the next night. He was nervous but stern. He reiterated what my parents had told me and said he was disappointed that I hadn't thought my actions through. I told him that it was important for people to be informed, and that I had hoped it would not only stir emotions but also cause others to act. John said I had always been compassionate and that that was a good thing. In this instance, however, sending the e-mail to his wife at work could have caused serious damage. I understood his argument and asked him what he wanted me to do. He asked for an apology, but I wasn't sorry.

I tried to get into a discussion about why he thought what I did was so wrong, but he didn't want to talk about that. My thoughts and opinions were no match for his age and experience. He told me I was too young to remember the pain Sara had caused the family and how badly she had hurt my parents. He said there were things I didn't understand or even know about. He was right. I was too young to remember. All I knew is what my sister had told me: Mom and Dad were hurt at first, then angry, sad, and confused, but they never stopped loving her. I wanted to ask him if he had spoken with them about this in the past ten years since they now seemed to be more accepting of her. I tried to interject but couldn't. The words were stuck in my throat, behind my own anger, sadness, and that choked-up, punched-in-the-stomach feeling. He told me he loved me and I managed to squeak, "I love you, too." We hung up. I knew our relationship would never be the same again.

I wasn't going to say anything to Sara about this. A few days later, however, after she found out what had happened from our sister, she called me. Sara told me not to worry about what John said. She usually ignored him when things such as this occurred and she thought I should too. He had always had a problem with her and there was nothing that would change his mind. I asked her about our other siblings and how they felt. She told me that no one had ever said much about it, but that everyone had responded a little differently. I wanted more detail.

Our oldest brother, Pat, took it in stride. He was closest to her while growing up, it never really seemed to phase him, and he rarely brought it up. Our youngest brother, James, the most religious of all of us, the same person who warned me about listening to "alternative" music because of its angry message, seemed surprised but was definitely tolerant. Donna had always been very understanding and the only one in the family with whom Sara spoke intimately before coming out to me.

Questions rattled in my head for days. How could five siblings, raised by the same parents, in the same town, and educated in the same county schools have such different reactions? Our older three siblings are separated by five years. I am twenty years younger than James. The generation gap between the others and me might help explain some of the differences, but it doesn't explain all of them.

I asked my parents why they thought everyone had such different attitudes, but they couldn't explain it either. They told me not to worry about it, to forget about my brother's phone call, and to move on. Sara had given me the same advice: "Forget about it. Ignore it. Don't worry about it." If we didn't talk about it, no problems would arise. No solutions would be found either. This was the same family policy that had kept me in the dark about Sara for so long.

I began combing the library for books and articles about reactions to a family member's coming out. Although I found a great deal on parents' responses, I could find very little on siblings' experiences. At the same time, I had been thinking about a possible thesis topic and a few of my professors agreed that this seemed to be a terrific opportunity to do something that was much needed. I thought about what they said, about my family's silence, and decided if no one else was going to talk about this issue, *I* would.

How has my sister's lesbianism affected me? I can honestly say that I wouldn't be where I am today if it weren't for her. Currently

I am working on my master's thesis, researching the reactions of siblings to their lesbian sisters' disclosure. My relationship with Sara has definitely grown since I found out. She trusts me, and I feel more comfortable discussing relationship issues with her than with anyone else in our family. We aren't just brother and sister. We're friends.

The most important way my sister has affected my life would be that she helped me to realize the privileges I have being a white, heterosexual male. She has endured prejudice and discrimination that I cannot imagine. Doors that never open for her have been wide open for me. She has struggled with the label of *different* or even *deviant* throughout her life. Although my political views are much more liberal than hers, and I am far more vocal, I have moved along in life with little resistance, thanks to my heterosexuality. Although I have often encountered people who aren't accepting of my ideas, they have generally been accepting of me. I often think back to my high school years and wonder: If I had known about her then, would I have been as vocal a supporter as I was in college? Would I have been supportive at all? Individuality is something I have always valued, but people often pay a high price for being different, especially in high school. If I had been gay friendlier in high school, would all of those doors have remained open for me?

My sister didn't choose to be a lesbian, and I didn't choose to be the brother of a lesbian. It just happened that way. I wouldn't change it for anything. Sara has taught me more by living her life and being herself than any class or book ever could. Without knowing it, she challenged me to face my fears and encouraged me to speak out against the silence that hinders the development of honest relationships between sexual minorities and the people who never try to know who they truly are.

– 13 –

My Sister's Closet

Meredith Greenfield Siegel

When my sister told me she was gay, it came as no great surprise. I don't even remember when I first realized it because, in some way, it was something I always knew. I couldn't have articulated it or completely understood what it meant, or what it would come to mean. It was just part of who she was—my kind, considerate, brilliant, generous, beautiful, thoughtful, analytical, critical, witty, acerbic, neat, loving, sweet, gay sister.

Beth, now forty-six, and I, now thirty-eight, grew up in a middle-class Brooklyn neighborhood. We lived in a three-room apartment in a lovely building where we shared a bedroom for the first nine years of my life. My mom had great taste and furnished our home with artwork and interesting antiques. She painted the hardwood floor of our bedroom a groovy shade of purple, then coated it with polyurethane so it was shiny. I liked sharing a room with my sister. I remember lying in the dark at night, talking and giggling together, both of us pretending to be asleep when our parents came in to check on us.

From there we moved to a brand-new three-family house nearby where we each had our own room. Beth was often responsible for me: baby-sitting if my parents went out; taking me to my dance and piano lessons. She took care of me.

When I was ten, Beth left home to attend college. I missed her. It felt odd without her. We spoke on the phone and wrote letters. I remember staying overnight in her dorm room once when our parents and I went to visit. I loved being there and finally getting to see what college was like. I felt close to her. During those summers, I went to sleep-away camp and we continued to write, getting to know each other in a very special way. By the time Beth graduated and came back home to live, I was fourteen and much more grown-up. In many ways, the age gap between us had closed considerably.

After she moved back, I noticed changes in her. She had become quite secretive, on edge, and often angry. Frankly, she intimidated me. She still tried to be available, but I definitely did not feel comfortable asking about her private life. I attributed it to her being stressed by having to live at home while she was in graduate school or to my being an annoyance. It was probably around this time that I figured out she was a lesbian. I honestly can't recall exactly how. Was it a phone conversation I overheard? A photo I saw in her room?

I attended a progressive high school, was involved in the theater department, and knew many gay students and teachers. Homosexuality was just not that big a deal among my friends. In some ways, my high school seemed more liberal than the college I went to, where not everyone was as comfortable with the issue. After a close friend of mine, one I had always assumed was gay, came out, my response was, "Yeah, so what do you have to tell me?" He was worried about what I might say because he had disclosed to a mutual, seemingly accepting friend and she had become upset.

In college, I took courses in sociology, joined the campus Women's Coalition, listened to "wimmin's" music, and participated in Take Back the Night marches. I quickly learned more about feminism and made some lesbian friends. It was sometime during college that Beth finally told me she was gay. I said I already knew. She was shocked and hurt and wondered why I had never said anything. I told her that I had figured when she wanted me to know, she would tell me. It hadn't occurred to me that she was in conflict about it. I deeply wish it had. We might have been closer then.

What I didn't know was that our mother had told her *not* to tell me. Apparently, she hadn't taken the news too well and was worried I would be upset, hurt, or damaged by this. If I had known what a difficult time my mom was giving her, I would have let on that I already suspected; I would have said it was fine with me and that I would not become a lesbian just because my big sister was one. (That I had to have a pair of matching suede desert boots and a plaid, diagonal, zip jacket similar to hers when I was little didn't mean we had to have matching sexual orientations as grown-ups.) I am sorry I wasn't able to make things easier for the two of them. I just didn't think of it as an issue that went beyond my sister and me.

That my mother had such a difficult time with it was a surprise. Being intelligent and progressive, she seemed open-minded about race and women's issues and the like. She always taught me that differences of all kinds shouldn't matter. I remember coming home from high school one day after talking with my friends about interracial dating. They were saying that their parents would be upset if they dated someone of a different race or even a different religion. I was so proud to say, "Oh, my mom is cool. She wouldn't care." When I told her how great I thought it was that she was free of prejudice, she hesitated a moment, smiled, agreed, and then nervously asked me if I was trying to tell her I was dating a black guy.

What my father's response to all of this was I couldn't say. It was not apparent at the time. If I had to venture a guess, I am sure that, being the sensitive man I know him to be, he probably found it quite upsetting to witness my sister and my mother going through this. Now he is accepting of Beth and warmly affectionate toward her partner of ten years, Ann. He is happy that his daughter is happy.

As my mother became increasingly ill in the last years of her own life, her perspective changed considerably. Similar to my father, she got to know and became quite fond of Ann. While she worried that discrimination might make Beth's life more difficult, she only wished for her daughter's happiness. My mother died in 1996.

As for me, the quality of my relationship with Beth is the most important thing—not her sexuality. As I become older, I realize that not everyone thinks the way I do. For the most part, I am truly comfortable with her lesbianism. All of my friends know. When casual acquaintances ask, "Is she married?" I mostly answer with the truth. Sometimes I hedge, trying to anticipate what their response will be. Those times I am not completely candid are based on the fear that I will have to deal with someone's narrow-minded, insensitive attitude. Am I trying to protect Beth, my children, myself?

My daughter, Ruby, now six, has always called Beth and her partner "the Aunts." She asks why my sister isn't married. I tell her that Beth has Aunt Ann, that they love each other, they love her, and they are her family. Although my sister would like me to be more specific, to use the word *lesbian* when I'm speaking with Ruby, I don't think this label is important right now. Perhaps she has a point though. Maybe I am not yet ready to talk about all of this with my daughter; maybe I am worried about how she will feel when she fully understands; maybe I want to help her avoid the possibility that one day somebody will say something hurtful to her—maybe all three.

My son, now almost three years old, likes Ruby to paint his fingernails and toenails and loves to wear her dress-up mules. If my sister weren't lesbian, would that have any resonance for me at all? Would I still wonder, Will he be gay?

Having a lesbian sister didn't make me question my own sexuality. It did, however, contribute to the development of my social consciousness, heighten my awareness of politics and prejudices, and encourage me to try to understand my family a bit more.

I love Beth very much. I am proud of her, thankful for her, and can't imagine life without her.

– 14 –

Knowing Sheila

Maggi Sullivan

Sheila was always the adventurous one. She smoked early, climbed trees, fought with boys, tried the convent, drove from New York to California in an Austin Healy Sprite, and lived and taught in Florida. The thing I admired most, even as a young girl, however, was that she was the first woman in our small-town parish to wear slacks to mass.

There are six children in our family—five girls and one boy, with a twenty-year span between the oldest and youngest. Sheila is the second child. As the youngest daughter, I didn't know her very well while growing up. She was gone on her adventures, and by the time she got back, we were both adults. She grew up and went to school in the nearby small city, whereas when I was in the first grade, we moved to the village my brother and I would grow up in. Our parents both worked; our father, a salesman, was gone most of the week; our mother was a teacher. We were rumored to have money, and all my friends were afraid of our father, who appeared gruff and demanding. Sheila was not afraid of him, though, and those adventures of hers proved it.

Perhaps the most daring adventure of all was the one he never knew about: her declaration, at age fifty-five, with a husband and two grown sons, that she was a lesbian. By that time, both our parents had died.

When I was doing some research on John Cheever for my master's thesis, I found several references from critics and his friends who felt, after Cheever's death, that clues to his bisexuality had

87

been in his writings all along—hindsight. There were no early clues for me about Sheila's lesbianism. I knew she had been a "searcher" of sorts—always happy to experience cultures and people and places; I knew she could live in the moment like nobody else; I knew she was giving and liberal and strong. I didn't know she was gay, but, as with Cheever's friends, looking back, it all fits.

The art of being direct was never mastered in our family. Clues would be randomly scattered in conversation, usually only after a cocktail or two. The night, about five years ago, when Sheila told us that she was a lesbian, my sisters and I were spending the weekend on the St. Lawrence River at my oldest sister Mary's place. Four of us stayed up after Mary had gone to bed. I remember distinctly that we were discussing music, and the conversation turned to k.d. lang as a favorite singer and persona. I also remember saying that, if I could imagine being sexual with another woman, k.d. would be the one. Sheila took it from there. I was so happy about her being direct, so thrilled that she had told us (and, possibly, I had enough of an alcohol buzz to react without the incumbent and requisite Irish melancholy), that my joy was what came through. It was only later that I started feeling angry and saddened by the knowledge that she had forced herself to live a role instead of a life for so many years. She never acted on her sexual orientation until after she came out to her husband and family. Only then, it seemed, did she really begin living.

So I asked her at one point if the "wasted years" made her angry or sad, but she assured me they didn't. I wondered how others, including friends, had reacted to the news. Our brother is a born-again Christian, and I don't think anyone has directly addressed this with him. He knows that after all those years of marriage, Sheila and her husband divorced amicably—not the first friendly divorce in our family. He has met Sheila's partner, but only during family parties with many distractions. He may have wondered to himself, but I don't believe he has let any conscious understanding come to the fore. Despite her having been an administrator in the small-town school system where we had lived since 1958, to Sheila's close friends, the knowledge makes no difference. I think my friends, though younger, were more shocked.

What Sheila's coming out did in terms of reexamining our family history and relations perhaps had the most effect on us as a family group. Suddenly, cousins who were always a bit "odd" came into focus as being either openly gay or repressed—even back a generation or two. It also seemed that during the next two or three years, people I knew were coming out in droves: co-workers of my husband; old school friends; students in my classes. I had known gay men and lesbians before, but, suddenly, the atmosphere had changed enough that people were less afraid to be open.

I know what this has all meant to me, and for the most part my other sisters have had similar responses: Sheila's coming out has only added another dimension to who she already is. Her sons accepted her announcement without tribulation. Her husband had a difficult time with it for a while, but, eventually, he, too, understood and moved on. They are still good friends—he comes to visit from Michigan where he lives with his new girlfriend. Sheila is involved in her grandchildren's lives and has found her niche in family law.

Our oldest sister, Mary, has always been more conservative in her politics than the rest of the family. Sheila was most nervous about telling her. To my mind, however, Mary has grown more tolerant in her later years. Although it took time, she has become more comfortable with Sheila's sexuality, which has, in turn, helped her be more understanding of others, including herself.

Being able to be a whole person has enriched all of the lives that Sheila has touched directly. The woman who used to suffer from daily pain in her neck and shoulders, from tension that we ascribed to her stressful job in education, has become smoother around the edges, extremely confident in her convictions, and utterly joyous in life. There is no greater ally of the confused and marginalized than one who has experienced, even privately, even quietly, those same states. This is the blessing we have received from watching Sheila. I hope our unconditional love for her has made this, her most important adventure, less trying.

– 15 –

The Older Kids

Tess Russo

"She'll never be with a man again." At first I was stunned by what my dad was saying about my older sister, Lee. I wondered how he knew. But as he continued to talk, I realized he was unaware of what she had told me only a couple of weeks before: that she had been involved with a woman for the past five months. Dad was referring to the fact that Lee had broken up with her long-term boyfriend, whom no one in the family had liked. We all breathed a collective sigh of relief, but none of us were prepared for her latest relationship, least of all me.

Twenty-five years earlier, when I was nineteen years old and struggling to come to terms with my own lesbianism, I had come out to Lee. Two years apart and the oldest ones of the family brood of six, we were fairly close while growing up. We had had three years to bond before our next sibling came along. After that, the remaining four were born in rapid succession. Because my sister and I were the older kids, we carried a lot of the responsibility for taking care of the younger kids as well as performing many of the household chores. We grew closer through commiseration. When I came out to Lee, I was looking for some much-needed support and understanding but, instead, was stung by her response: that she did not want my partner and me to be together around her young children. Her lack of trust made me feel even more ashamed of the lesbian self I was trying to embrace.

Over time, her position softened and we were able to restore the mutually supportive relationship that had been severed. I can't help being aware of the contrast between Lee's response when I came out to her and my response when she came out to me. At a large family gathering, she took me aside and said, "I'm involved with a woman. Can you recommend any good books on lesbian sex?" That was absolutely the last thing I ever expected her to say. It went against everything I knew about her. She was the epitome of little Susie Homemaker. Her beliefs were traditional, even somewhat conservative. She had dependent relationships with men, striving to fit the traditional feminine mold. Even her outfits, down to her shoes, were *always* well coordinated. Involved with a woman? Well, that just didn't fit.

After staring at her, too shaken to know what to say, she told me, "You can close your mouth now." Stalling for time so that my brain could catch up, I admitted I was shocked but happy for her. But as soon as I said the word, I realized I wasn't exactly sure I *was* happy. Besides the fact that Lee didn't conform to my notion of what a lesbian was (I, of course, always looked and acted the part), I wondered how this would affect my role as "the lesbian of the family." I had fought long and hard to gain acceptance from my parents and siblings, and my lifetime partner, Lori, and our two children had been basking in their support for a number of years. Would this rock the boat? Would two lesbians in the family be one lesbian too many? I felt apprehensive about the possible consequences.

I confess: I was dying to meet Kay, my sister's girlfriend. Based on what I was told, I pictured someone similar to my sister— ultrafemme—perhaps experiencing her first relationship with a woman. So I made up an excuse to drop by Lee's apartment. Surprise! I'd had it all wrong and rushed home to tell Lori: "She's butch. Soft-butch, but definitely butch!" I was delighted. Butch-femme relationships—now *that* I understood.

As the months went by, I wondered when Lee would tell the rest of the family. By then, she and Kay had done the "lesbian thing"— moved in together, merging their households of two dogs and two cats. It had to be obvious to everyone, I thought. Two women in their forties making a home together? I had been merging households with women for years. I offered to come out to our parents for her. She declined.

A few weeks later, Lee and my partner, Lori, met at my mother and father's house to do some wallpapering for them. Unbeknownst to Lori, Lee decided that right then and there was the time to tell my parents. Oblivious to what was going on in the other part of the house, Lori went about preparing the walls for the paper. She was suddenly caught in the very awkward position of trying to soothe both my mom and dad, who were shocked after my sister blurted out her news, then abruptly left. (Fortunately, my partner forgave my sister and still speaks with her.) At the time, my parents didn't have a clue about Lee, nor did any of our siblings. It was interesting to hear their reactions. Though none of them seemed particularly upset, they all thought that being a lesbian just didn't "fit" who they thought Lee was, which was how I felt too.

Lee and Kay will soon be celebrating six years together. I'm surprised it's lasted this long, but I can honestly say that I *am* happy now when I see them together and see how much their relationship has grown. Lori and I don't socialize with them as much as I thought we might, but we all see one another regularly at family gatherings. It took a while for everyone genuinely to welcome Kay into the fold, but now that she is part of the family, we expect her to be at all our get-togethers and miss her when she is not there.

My fears concerning Lee's relationship with a woman negatively impacting my own position within the family never materialized. Our roles did not change from "the older kids" to "the lesbians." I've learned that being a daughter and a sister carry a lot more weight than being a lesbian.

My sister is not completely "out" and probably doesn't even consider herself a lesbian, but rather just a woman who happens to be in a relationship with another woman. She does not advertise her lesbianism, and from her appearance, you would never suspect it. There are no rainbow stickers on her car or rainbow flags flying from her porch. In most respects, she has remained true to the image we have always had of her.

Although it is probably difficult for her, I feel proud when she attends family events with Kay by her side. However, I am still startled when occasionally I see Lee at exclusively lesbian events, since I had come to view these as "family-free zones." I am happy to see her, though, and thrilled to share my world with her. I remember how difficult all of this was for me at first, and I like to think I paved the way. I've learned a lot from my sister, but I never expected she would be the one to challenge my own lesbian bias.

16

Look What You've Done to Me

Terry Dolney

At age fifty-five, I've managed to push most of the unpleasant memories from childhood and adolescence out of my mind. Back then, I felt lonely and hurt much of the time, frequently withdrawing from the world. Although I'm finding it difficult to remember the past, it feels as if I need to try. I know that writing can be cathartic, so I'm going to look on this as an opportunity.

I am the oldest child in a family of ten. Besides me, my mother and biological father had Jeff, who is two years younger. Our father was in and out of our lives for many years. When I was fourteen, my mother had twins—Tina and Tim—on Christmas morning. Our mother finally decided it was not "better to stay married for the kids' sake," and he was gone before the twins came home from the hospital. On many levels, it was a relief to have him out. But because of my emotional distance from my mother and brother, both of whom were closer to each other than they were to me, I reached out to my dad. I got rejected—many times. We have not had contact in years.

The twins brought love into my life, something with which I was totally unfamiliar. I was unable to figure out if I played the role of mother, sister, or both. I was unprepared to be good at either. Somehow I knew right from the beginning that a special relationship between Tina and me would evolve.

When the twins were toddlers, our mother met John. He had a son, J.T., who was thirteen, the same age as Jeff, and a daughter,

Cheryl, age eight. He was a widower and needed child care; our mother was a divorcée and needed support. Since they seemed to have fun together, they made the best of it and eventually married. Several years later, they had Andy. Because our biological father denied paternity of the twins, though we all believed he *was* their biological father, John legally adopted them. We were always being reminded what a "savior" John was: "What a good man—taking in all those kids." The truth is, John turned out to be not so good and quite abusive, particularly to Tina, who revealed that to me many years later, further solidifying the bond between us.

I married at age twenty-eight and gave birth to three children in two and a half years. Having so many in quick succession made it that much harder to learn how to be a parent. My mother couldn't or, more accurately, wouldn't help me. She was done with parenting. Tina, only a teenager then, came to my rescue many times. She baby-sat, cleaned my house, and understood me way before I figured myself out.

Tina and I were in and out of each other's lives for the next few years. I moved around the country and she eventually left southern California for Massachusetts. After graduating with honors from Fullerton State, she went to study at MIT (Massachusetts Institute of Technology). We were all so proud of her. She brought her longtime boyfriend, Ray, home for Christmas that year. We expected she would marry him and have the babies she always wanted. Privately, Tina asked me what I thought about the possibility of her marrying Ray, even if she didn't feel he was totally "right" for her. Surprised by her question, I told her she should probably feel more certain before making such an important decision.

To our great surprise, Tina flew from Cambridge to California one weekend some time after this (I'm not exactly sure how long after), proceeded separately to tell Mom, then each sibling, that she was in love with a woman and that *this* felt "right" to her. I had moved to Oregon by then but was in California on business. When she disclosed this to me, I shed tears of happiness—happy that she was happy. She handed out copies of articles and books that would help us understand her and quickly left to participate in an AIDS conference in San Francisco. (By that time, she had received her master's degree and was involved in research aimed at testing new AIDS medications.) I was totally comfortable with her "news." (I swear I had dreamed about it the night before.) The only question I had was whether she was still planning on having babies, knowing how important this had always been for her. She reassured me, and herself, that she thought she could make it all work.

After Tina came out, we all had a fleeting thought that "some big macho dyke in leather with tattoos and studs" had somehow convinced her that men were bad. My mother had met Tina's girlfriend, Jenny, on a previous visit to Massachusetts; she was introduced to my mom at the time as Tina's "college friend." Mom was glad Tina had Jenny, easing those initial fears of ours.

Thereafter, my new role was to be a mother to my own mother. She was always so strong about everything, but this upset and confused her: "What did I do wrong? Am I to blame? Don't they say this comes from a weak father and overbearing mother? I can't say my family is perfect anymore." One gift—one of many—that Tina gave me was a new relationship with my mother. As I got information on PFLAG (Parents, Families and Friends of Lesbians and Gays) and other support groups, I began to learn a lot. Mom and I talked endlessly about this new phase of our lives but were concerned about how each sibling would handle it. We were, and continue to be, quite surprised by some of their initial and later reactions.

My oldest brother, Jeff, and his wife took it in stride: "Oh, I guess our kids will be okay. Just act like everything is fine and it will be." Even though J.T. has had much turmoil in his own life, he said to Tina, "We loved you before as an intelligent and wonderful sister. Why would we feel differently now?"

Our stepsister, Cheryl, initially presented more of a problem. She has had two marriages and one long-term relationship, each of which failed. After she divorced her second husband, she became very religious and would go on and on about how homosexuality was a "sin" and how she did not want her daughter around Aunt Tina. I acted as a buffer between Cheryl and Mom, who at the time didn't have the strength or the knowledge to "defend" Tina or herself. Cheryl has since opened up her heart and mind and now totally accepts Tina.

Our biggest worries centered on the youngest, Andy, who's attitude turned out to be "What's the problem?" He was a senior in high school at the time and totally nonjudgmental. Although Tim, Tina's twin, initially told us he thought we were all just ignorant, scared, confused, and needed only to be educated about homosexuality, later his attitude changed dramatically. He now accepts a literal interpretation of the Bible and is completely intolerant. It's very upsetting for me to see him put on a front around Tina, trying to act as if everything is fine. When she is not around, he ridicules her.

Even though Tina and I are physically distant, we continue to be emotionally close. Except for our sexualities, we are alike in many ways, despite the different circumstances in which we grew up and the difference in our ages.

What about the present? Tina and Jenny have been together now for thirteen years and have two wonderful children, both through artificial insemination. Jenny then went through a second-parent adoption. They are an amazing, "normal" family living in the San Francisco area. Jenny is, and has always been, my favorite sister-in-law.

As for myself, I became interested in gay rights a few years after moving to Oregon in 1988 and was confronted by the views of Lon Maybon and his OCA (Oregon Citizens Alliance). He had been trying for years to get state measures passed that would continue to make homosexual behavior illegal and discrimination possible. Although I had always been very shy, especially in large groups, I was so upset about the OCA and what it stood for that I was determined to stand up and fight: I became active in our local grassroots organization; I petitioned at the state capitol; I even found myself on the evening news. Our efforts went on for several years. Even though the OCA has lost credibility, the Christian right has unfortunately gained strength. They now promote a "Save Our Children" campaign, trying to make it a crime even to mention the word *homosexuality* to students.

Since I was not employed during that period of my life, spurred on by Tina's work on the HIV vaccine, I decided to volunteer with the local HIV Prevention Task Force and, through that, became involved with and eventually ran a county-based nonprofit program for people with HIV/AIDS. Through this program, we were then able to build Swan House, a specialized care unit for low-income people living with HIV/AIDS. It opened three years ago and I am on the board of directors and a volunteer with the residents.

Over four years ago, I started to work for the county health department as an HIV counselor in settings as diverse as jails, mental health clinics, and drug and alcohol programs. I absolutely love it. It's my passion. Unfortunately, the funds are drying up and I don't know how much longer I will have a job. Without having been exposed to people who are different from me, I probably would not have been as open and accepting, and I definitely would not have ever sought a job such as this one.

Clearly Tina has been a major force in my life, and it doesn't end with just me. My three children and husband have all learned from Tina's example; we all do what we can to bring fairness and equality to everyone. With a smile on my face, I occasionally say to Tina, "Look what you've done to me!" Without her, I would never be where I am or who I am.

17

Common Threads

Ann McWhorter

I did not much mind taking a backseat to Dell. She was, after all, the big sister, and she usually liked me. It was 1967 in Alabama. It was steaming hot all the time, except when it was so cold that Dell and I huddled in front of the space heater, taking turns getting the most direct heat as we changed, limb by limb, from pajamas to church clothes.

At just over two years my senior, boyish, seven-year-old Dell was the only other small person in the house. My parents said she was a genius. She went to school during the day while I stayed home with Mama. When she came home, she became engrossed in books for hours on end, sometimes stopping to play with race cars or Lincoln Logs. But if I was very, very accommodating, agreeing to do all the cleanup, she would reward me by playing Barbies with me or by cutting out paper doll families with me from the Sears catalog.

Though Dell was as excellent a Barbie doll player as she was a reluctant one, she excelled at being Ken. It was important back then for the smartest, most creative girl to be the animator of Ken. Ken did everything. He decided when he and Barbie would go out and what they would do. He made the phone calls and led the conversations. If marriage was to be proposed, he proposed it. Without a good Ken, Barbie could do little more than change outfits.

Since Dell was so smart, and better, it made sense for her to play the boy in all of our games. Boys always had the smarter, better role. They were soldiers, firemen, and rescuers of damsels tied to railroad tracks. Girls waited faithfully at home, cheered on the boys, or clung to them adoringly, saying, "My hero!"

When Dell was very small, according to old photographs, our mother had dressed her in frilly frocks and put little bows in her blonde hair. I remember when we both still wore "stand-out slips" that were scratchy beneath our Sunday dresses. But as the years passed, Dell's wishes were increasingly honored. Her hair was cut short; her jeans were bought in the boys' department and had zippers in front. I, in contrast, wore neon flowered pants with the zipper in back, grew my fingernails as long as possible before getting sent to clip them off, and sashayed with the occasional boa thrown over one shoulder. On Christmas and birthdays, whatever the gift, I got the pink or red one, and Dell got the blue one.

It appeared to me that the whole family came to support, silently, Dell's increasingly androgynous style. Thus, my femininity became, to me, increasingly indicative of my inferiority to her and to the rest of the family. In a family that shunned fashion and frivolity, I was aligned with all things pink and superficial. When I spoke, with reticence, my parents said I was just "talking to hear my head rattle," but my hero, my big sister, of whom I was the biggest fan, was, in my mind, held in reverent awe by the whole family—except maybe Mary.

Our big sister, Mary, was a senior in high school. She spent long hours hunched over hieroglyphic textbooks, popping gum, and making stripes with a yellow highlighter. She had a scholarship to Vanderbilt, where she planned to study medicine, then take her skills overseas to save the world. I think we always knew that, whatever Mary did in life, she would not come back to Alabama.

Mary held a grudge—a grudge against the family, the society, the South, and aspects of each that were too much bother for her to explain. That grudge seemed to extend even to blonde little Dell, who had entered Mary's world when Mary was nine. In 1967, high school girls were not permitted to wear pantsuits, and Mary wore the requisite dresses with her grudge on her sleeve, moving about with the grace of a lumberjack. She called me Bug because I could not always wait until her studying ended before soliciting her attention. I was honored to receive a nickname, such as it was. She did not seem to bear me any grudge at all and even occasionally took the time to teach me something from her books.

Aaron, our only brother, was already away in college in Birmingham. I was immensely proud of him. He was tall and handsome and smelled of the cigarettes he pretended not to have started smoking. He dated grown-up girls, occasionally bringing one home. I was intrigued and wished to know them, looking at them for clues to femininity.

I searched everywhere for clues. When Cissy on the TV sitcom *Family Affair* brushed her hair 100 strokes before bedtime, I did the same. When the Brady girls spent too much time in the bathroom, irking the Brady boys, I locked myself in our bathroom for as long as I could stand to stay. Eventually I grew tired of making potions out of old shampoo and talcum powder and had to come out. When Marcia Brady talked too long on the phone, my friend Kathy and I tied up the line as long as we could, playing a full game of Monopoly on two separate boards. I did impressions of Mae West, inviting male visitors to "come up and see me sometime." I whirled around in pretty skirts, my affected airs earning me the disapproving name "Miss Priss" from Mama.

Mama was a constant presence in my world, like the white noise of traffic at the intersection just outside our small, brick ranch house. She sewed from before dawn to past dark, except on Sundays. While the sewing machine whirred, she watched her soap operas religiously. I played soap operas with my Barbies and Kens on the floor of my room, concealing their illicit conduct, which would have been visible only upon inspection of my imagination—a feat of which I feared Mama might be capable.

Daddy was the only one who liked it when I whirled in pretty skirts, but he was gone most of the time, working second shift and overtime in blue coveralls with a number on his chest. He carried a black lunchbox every day, always containing the same two roast beef and mayonnaise sandwiches, Fritos, and a Moon Pie. Mama told me often that he was depressed and would have preferred to die, but that he had to live for us, to toil double-time at his miserable job just to feed and clothe the five of us. When Daddy was home, he slept. We had to be very quiet lest we rouse the snoring giant and face his wrath. Usually, he was not interested in us, the children, and spelled that out plainly and regularly, taking care, as did Mama, not to spare the rod and spoil the child or allow us to "get the big head" that attention and affection might breed. But sometimes when he awoke in a good mood on a Saturday, we could run in the room, hop on Pop, and hear stories of when he was a "bad wittle boy."

Mama and Daddy presented a flawlessly unified front to the children. It was many years before I realized that they might not be in perfect agreement on every point. To the day Mama died, recently, I never even heard them exchange cross words. Likewise, they conveyed to their children, without a word, that no hint of disrespect could be tolerated. In my memory, that unspoken rule went unchallenged, and the consequences of breach remain a mystery.

Mama's respect for the unspeakable permeated relations with the world outside our walls. Women from the neighborhood and church often came or called. Mama sat sipping coffee, listening as the middle-aged daughter of the Klansman across the street gave her the latest news from the John Birch Society, explaining the evils of desegregation, that the women's libbers wanted unisex bathrooms, and who else, as it turned out, was a Communist. Mama smiled sweetly, her dissent imperceptible. When at last her visitor was gone, Mama took Excedrin. She lay on the sofa, with the lights out, and praised my soft little hands as I massaged her forehead to make the ache go away. When it didn't hurt too bad, she told me her deep, dark dangerous secrets—that she opposed the Vietnam War, supported civil rights, supported women's liberation, and believed in the equality and dignity of all people. I promised, silently, not to tell.

Mama was an anomaly. Born into rural poverty in Alabama, she grew up with bigotry as a given. All by herself, using her own good sense and the teachings of the church, she reasoned that it was wrong. She often told Dell and me, "The only people I'm prejudiced against are prejudiced people."

Daddy grew up with relative prosperity, the son of a sharp-dressing businessman. His parents were self-educated in art and literature. His father was impressive, but arrogant and pedantic, and abusive of Daddy, whom he treated dismissively as mere farm labor and whom he made feel unintelligent. Daddy's father had joined the Ku Klux Klan when it was fashionable but dropped out when the klavern determined to find and beat a white woman who allegedly had been intimate with a black man. Yet he declared to his own daughter that if she ever "carried on" with a black man— not the word he used for the race—he would kill her himself.

Daddy had never questioned the segregation and bigotry around him until one day in the 1940s, when as a young army recruit in Washington, DC, about to sail to Europe, he saw a black soldier at a lunch counter. When the waitress refused to serve the soldier, the soldier left in a fury, knocking the shakers and condiments off the countertop. Daddy instantly empathized. He instantly understood the injustice. That day, he became a permanent convert to the civil rights movement without ever having heard of it.

Daddy never uttered a word of his convictions to his parents. Sunday after Sunday, Mama and Daddy loaded Dell and me into the old Chevrolet station wagon and headed out to the countryside, to the old mock-plantation home where Daddy's parents lived. While Dell read yellowed books from the shelves and I coaxed wild kittens outside the screen door, Daddy's father droned on at the kitchen table, quoting Shakespeare and the segregationists in turn. Daddy listened and seethed. In the car going home, he binged on Rolaids.

We were little, attentive people, Dell and I, in this world of the unspeakable. We learned not to speak before we learned to talk.

When we were little more than babies, our family had come under threat by the Klan. I always secretly wished that the threats had followed some heroic outspoken act by my parents. Instead, as best I can reconstruct, the threats were inspired by two converging events, innocent of heroic intent.

On August 6, 1964, the local newspaper printed a letter to the editor from my brother, Aaron, then seventeen, complete with his full name and address. I found it recently in my mother's things, yellowed and torn. In part he wrote:

> This year has seen churches bombed, our President assassinated, an innocent traveler shot down on a highway, and three civil rights workers murdered. . . . These premeditated acts are the products of fear controlled men. . . . Many of us, who

were born with the capacity to love as well as to hate, have chosen to fear hatred itself so much that we will remain silent rather than risk our own security. . . . Truly the Christian cannot condone hatred or any organization based on this destroyer. He cannot allow such as these to go unchallenged. Fear unchallenged is fear unleashed. The . . . Ku Klux Klan breed[s] on hatred and thrive[s] on fear. We who would be Christians must meet fear face to face and hatred hand in hand.

For some time before the letter was published, my parents and a few other couples were planning the creation of a new Methodist church in the growing area of town where they had built our home in 1958. The earliest services of that church were held in our living room. False rumors spread that the new, white congregation intended to integrate the church. So on August 6, 1964, when the son of these suspected integrationists spoke naively against the Klan—a group he could not really believe held sway or even had a real-life following—the calls started. Among the threats, the callers said they would kill the baby girls.

Mama was thirty-seven, still a lanky, dark beauty, an eager-to-please and insecure only child whose parents had divorced when she was two and then both died young, leaving her an orphaned new bride in a world as small as home and church. With Daddy working second shift at the plant, she found herself alone every night with four children, locking doors and closing curtains, hoping the threats were a bluff. It went on for some time. Daddy still remembers, after a telephone call at midnight one night, waiting for hours in a locked car in our open carport, gun in hand, daring the Klan to come try to hurt his family.

And so we learned to be closeted. Before Dell and I understood the particulars of what all the fuss was about, we had learned that we were vulnerable; we had learned that loose lips, or even unpopular thoughts not well concealed, if they touch a nerve, invite the ever-lurking possibility of violence.

Dell's being easily and often mistaken for a boy, however, did not touch a nerve. Though it persisted into her teens, it was about tomboyishness, clumsiness maybe, or perhaps even envy of masculine prerogative, but it was not about sexuality. The concept of anyone being a lesbian was to bud early in Dell's private thoughts, but it certainly had not occurred to my parents or me in 1967.

I did know soon enough what "gay" meant. I asked Mama once, straight out, when Mary Tyler Moore seemed so sad that the man she was dating turned out to be gay. I was lying on the floor in front of the television with my head on a pillow and turned back to look at Mama in her rocking chair. She explained that "gay" is when a man prefers the company of other men to the company of women. I thought that described most Alabama and Auburn football fans, and I wondered why that would make Mary Tyler Moore feel sad. I turned back to the television, though, and left it at that.

Eventually, of course, I had a better understanding. So did the Methodist Church, which issued from on high an official, warm welcome of some sort to homosexual Methodists. My parents, stalwart, moral, though quiet supporters of equality and justice for all, supported the church's position, but we didn't know anybody gay—well, except for one male cousin, but that was just hushed speculation.

Mama did not, however, support asking and certainly not telling. She did not even support acting on a homosexual impulse. The problem with homosexuality, unlike all the other personal attributes to which bigotry might attach, was that it related directly to *sexuality*.

Most dreadful of all sins was sex outside of marriage. If in 1967 I had little clue what sex was, I certainly knew it would kill my mother if I did it. She did her maternal job of conveying that her love for me was unconditional insofar as I could murder and she would still visit me in jail. "I would be very disappointed, but I would still love you," she said. But love or no love, all would be lost in a spontaneous combustion of burning shame should I ever do *something*—and that something had to do with where babies come from.

Once when Dell was in school and I was the only one to accompany Mama on the drive to her annual Pap smear, I stood on the car seat—as children did back then—and listened, puzzled and worried. Someone was having a baby, and Mama thought her mother must be ashamed, because it was a terrible thing. On and on the story went, until finally I said, "But Mama, I thought you *liked* babies."

Mama demanded abstinence outside marriage from both sexes. For females of all ages, she also demanded absence of interest. Good girls didn't think about, want, or like sex. Bad girls didn't really like it either, but they were pitiful creatures looking for love. When they weren't her own daughters, God forbid, she could extend her Christian love and generosity in their direction and feel sorry for them.

Mama was confused and upset, though, by the soap operas she couldn't stop watching. Increasingly, in the 1960s and then in the 1970s, a soap opera woman would have sex with first one and then another man, other characters would be aware of it, and still they would comment admiringly that she was a wonderful person. Mama was beside herself time and again, distressed by the "immorality," and perplexed at the changing society that did not even bother anymore to articulate that it disagreed with her. She obsessed over sexual immorality aloud to me so often at such an early age, it was no wonder my dolls led soap opera lives. The more Mama obsessed, the more I obsessed, and the more important it was that she not read my imagination; she could not be allowed to know for sure that I, too, was bad, similar to the soap opera people, and that I probably would not go to heaven. No one, not even Dell, could know. When it was quiet at night, I felt especially desolate knowing that God, who was everywhere, *could* read my imagination and so did not like me at all.

Since, for Mama, sexuality was not, among decent people, a driving force in relationships, it was quite problematic for her to try to be accepting, as her ethics said she must, of homosexual people. As she articulated to me in my teen years, any sex they had was, by definition, outside of marriage, so they must have no sex. Since as decent people they didn't desire sex, so the logic would connect, abstinence should be no problem. All that being so, they certainly did not need to have parades or otherwise announce in any way any sexual fact about themselves. It was as simple as that, though, when she thought about it, Mama was still troubled and dissatisfied with her answers. That was okay, though, because it wasn't, as was race, an ever-present issue. It was all fairly theoretical, since we did not know anyone gay, except maybe that one cousin.

Meanwhile, Dell emerged from a troubled childhood full of phobias, to have in middle school the coolest best girlfriend ever. Kay offered me new clues to femininity. She dressed as Cher when Dell dressed as Sonny. She painted her nails red and sprayed on too much perfume, so that the furry cuffs of her winter coat were irreparably soaked through with Chanel No. 5. She bragged that all the boys were after her and tried to teach me the art of seduction. Kay and Dell slept together in Dell's bed weekend after weekend, wrestling and giggling and touching at every turn. A thought occurred to me once, "They act like boyfriend and girlfriend," but I brushed it off as impossible. Eventually Kay became enmeshed with the boy she later married, and she was not to be seen again.

Dell was by this time in high school. I had learned in the interim, since 1967, that I, too, was smart and far from superficial, but still I looked up to her as my superior. I tried not to notice that I had overtaken her in the social world—that though I was unusual in my own ways, which my peers could surely enumerate, I was generally regarded, at least by comparison, as a basically normal girl. She, on the other hand, was increasingly marginal. She was still an adult magnet, attracting mentors left and right in a way I never could. Still it was embarrassing to be asked, after walking with her to school, whether that boy with whom I had been walking was my new boyfriend. I maintained her place high on a pedestal by telling myself that these local peers of ours, whose opinions had never mattered to me any more than those of another species, simply could not see that this idiot of the feminine was my very own savant, a special, important, extraordinary person of whom I was still almost entirely proud.

She was challenging, though. We spent hours and hours together, her reading aloud to me from some book she loved, or the two of us singing parts from *Jesus Christ Superstar,* she King Herod, and I, Mary Magdalene. Then I'd leave to fulfill the bribe that bought me time with her, to make her a peanut butter and apple butter sandwich, and I'd come back to a locked door with darkness beneath. "Dell? Dell, can I come in?" "No, go away!" she'd say. Her mood had turned. I'd try one more time and then say, "Okay," as cheerfully as I could. She spent more and more time locked away in the dark, and she never would tell me what was wrong.

I thought I should know what was wrong. I thought something was wrong with our family, and everyone understood it but me. Aaron had long since evaded the draft and lived in a communal apartment in Toronto. He had issues with the family that he never explained to me. Mary had moved away and estranged herself from our parents off and on, never explaining to me what exactly her overriding grievance was. And Dell hinted that there were horrible things she couldn't explain to me. Clearly I was not as smart as the rest of them and just couldn't quite see the obvious. I trusted they were right, since I was the "average" child, but to preserve my intellectual integrity, I decided to remain faithful to our parents until I matured enough to understand why I should not.

High school wore on, and Dell plummeted. One day during her senior year, I came home from school, and she was gone. I was greeted in the carport by my father's sister. Mama had checked Dell into a mental health facility at Dell's request. Aunt Rose offered me comfort, said it must be hard for me. I pushed that offer away; I could not accept it. Dell was suffering in some secret way. Mama and Daddy were suffering. I was just the sister.

Dell never went back to high school. Over the next few months, we saw her at the occasional family therapy session at the hospital. As far as I can recall, nothing helpful or explanatory was ever said. The psychiatrist blamed our parents mercilessly, brutally, for unnamed mistakes and shortcomings. Dell got thinner and thinner and more and more scrunched up in her chair, as if trying to burrow into it, speechless, her eyes downcast. Mama and Daddy, whom I had never seen cry, grew more and more tearful, breaking down often in front of me, killing me inside.

As Dell plummeted, my status in the family began to rise. I was now, and forever more have been, the only member of the family with whom everyone else communicated. Mama and Daddy began to rely on me to take calls from Dell, who would not speak to them, and relate whatever information seemed ethical to me to relate. More important, they let me know every day that I was their salvation. I was the only one who would never hurt them, the only one who made them feel that they were good parents, the only one who showed them love. And so, they said, they loved me—maybe (if it weren't a bad thing for a parent to do) even *best*.

My status did not rise at school. Some of my peers said that since I had a crazy sister, they couldn't go out with me anymore.

I learned many things in those months. I learned that my parents would never be there to save me no matter how much I hurt. I learned that I was there to save them, and maybe other people, and that therein lay my worth. I learned that even if I got smart enough to understand why I should abandon my parents, I never could. I learned that Dell valued me and needed me, and that I would never leave her either. I learned that I *was* somebody, after all, even if I was girlish. But I did not learn that Dell was gay. I did not learn, for years, that on the morning she went to the hospital, refusing Mama's urging to get out of bed long after I had left for school, she had secretly decided to kill herself. Unbeknownst to me, her sister, and maybe the closest person to her in the world, she had decided that day would be the day that she would die. Then she thought again, for a long time, and decided she could always die later and ought at least to give the hospital a try.

While the psychiatrist was bleeding my parents of all of their insurance and then personal funds, and of all of their self-esteem, he was, I later learned, bullying Dell to stop being a lesbian, trying to force-feed her heterosexuality.

Finally, he was arrested on drug charges, but Dell was gone by then. Mama and Daddy were losing their minds in confusion, trying to distinguish up from down, truth from extortion, having no idea what to believe, for what to repent, or what to do next. Daddy finally decided to stop paying the hospital. Dell left on her own, without speaking to our parents, moved to Birmingham, and got a job. She started college in the fall.

Two years later, I joined her there. She was a long-haired, anorexic rebel, infamous for taking on the school administration regularly. Upon my arrival, on scholarship, as was she, I was greeted by a swarm of people expecting me to be like her. I felt disappointingly ordinary. I never rebelled significantly in four years there. I was

merely a silent supporter of Dell's causes, always feeling inadequate because I did not fully understand them.

When I met my husband, I thought he was wonderful. I knew
someone else wonderful, and so determined that he and Dell
should meet. She was away at Oxford, so I had time to get to know
him well before that anticipated fateful day when I could introduce one special, important, extraordinary person to another and
let them ride off into the sunset. Before she returned, he finally
convinced me that he was not interested in her; he was interested
in me.

Dell kept me in the dark about her sexuality for many years
more. She told me all about her boyfriends as well as her women
friends, reversing the salient details. She once confided to me that
she was disturbed that some particularly malicious college boys
were calling her a lesbian and had invited her to a party in an attempt, she feared, to lure her into a setup for a violent attack. She
was hurt, she said, that they would think she was a lesbian. I tried
my best to listen sympathetically to this alien problem of being
falsely mistaken for gay, having no idea that in fact she was gay.

Dell went on to graduate school, where she met a man who
seemed to be her perfect intellectual match. For a time, she was reunited with our parents. Much as I had found that there was less
tension in my relationship with Mama once I was lawfully wed,
and so would likely not be a source of shame and doom for her, so
Dell and Mama both felt happier at last when Dell confided to
Mama that she had met a wonderful man at Vanderbilt, handsome,
smart, and so forth. The rejection that had so pained Mama was
eased, and Dell had a mother again who knew her, I thought.

Soon after, Mama suffered a massive stroke. She never knew
again that any of her history with Dell, good or bad, had ever happened. She knew only that she had a daughter named Dell whom
she loved, as she loved Daddy, Aaron, Mary, and me. I dressed
Mama for Dell's wedding in pretty, pale green silk, and the photographs barely reveal that the mother of the bride was totally blind
and totally lost.

Years later, after I had graduated from Harvard and was practic-
ing law in Boston, I got a letter. In several pages, Dell told me she
was gay and asked me if I could accept her. I hadn't wondered, so

good had Dell been at feeding me false impressions. Hearing the truth at that moment, though, I knew it to be the truth. I knew, in a flood of memories, what had been true all along. I knew about Kay and about a college professor. I knew that part of the pain and secrecy had been about the secret of her sexuality. Dell was coherent to me—the little girl, the teenager, the college student—for the first time, and I hadn't even been consciously aware until then how incoherent it all had been before.

I, too, had grown up with that family in that place. I firmly believed our parents and siblings were not homophobic and would not have disowned Dell. But I also bore the deep imprint of that burning taboo surrounding sexuality of any sort. I, too, had lived my whole life with the shame of secretly having sexuality. I also knew the absolute power of the unspeakable.

I told Dell immediately that, of course, I would accept her. Of course, of course, of course. She told me that she had come out to some friends and that they said it didn't make any difference to them. I told her it made a huge difference to me. How could it make no difference to me when it made all the difference in the world to her? How could it be nothing of consequence to me when it could have killed her? When it—being gay in the context of our world and time—gave her a life bound and gagged, unknowable to the people closest to her. When it meant she was hurt time and time again by hurtful words aimed at homosexuality, and so her personally, without the ability to mention it to anyone at all. When she had been unable to tell her sister for whom it was, among her girl and boy friends, that she really yearned and for whom she did not. When she had been unable to take a real date to an event. When she had lived much of her life unable to be genuine. I had felt just enough of it myself—the secrecy and shame—to know its power in an instant. And though I had always been open-minded on the subject, I became a fervent convert in that moment to civil rights of a kind still not fully advanced to this day.

So for the most part, the news of Dell's sexuality was happy news because it rang true and fit. It was also happy news for me for a very personal reason. I had felt demeaned in our family for being feminine. I was nearly masculine in contrast to the self-deprecating, affected feminine ideal in Alabama at the time, but in my home I was a veritable traitor to my gender, obviously not bright, not serious, selling out to the patriarchy. Added to that was a strong suggestion that I might be in danger of becoming a "bad girl." Mary, who recalls helping Mama to raise me, had adopted only sons, wanting nothing to do with girl children. And here was one of my sisters, whom I assumed had no use for my kind, telling me she *did* like girls, even *femme* girls, a lot! It was such a relief, so affirming.

When Dell gave me this news, she was estranged, as she is today, from the rest of the family. I continued to play my role, relating whatever information it seemed ethical to relate to our father, who waits with interest for each bit of news. I did not, however, "out" Dell, as it seemed not to be my business to do so. I felt it would be pointless gossiping, of no benefit to Daddy or Dell, possibly needlessly hurtful to Daddy, or that it might be all those things, and if it were, in retrospect, it could not be retracted. Leaving out that one fact meant leaving out half the explanation of Dell's divorce. It meant omitting the fact that Dell does not live alone now but rather has united with a female partner in a wonderful wedding in which my husband, daughter, and I participated. It meant leaving out all the other true characterizations about Dell's generally happy life and well-being that cannot be shared without sharing the fact that Carol is part of her life every single day.

Daddy is old and feeble. He cared for Mama at home for eighteen years. A few months ago he said he wanted Dell back. He had said it before many times in different ways, but a few months ago it was different. He is a man of few words, and he repeated it: "I want Dell back." I was with him in Florida, walking to the car. His words hit me.

It isn't that Dell is gone from him because Dell is gay. I don't think I can articulate why Dell is gone from him. I could write volumes about why, but I don't know why, fundamentally. I don't fundamentally know why Mary is gone either, and she isn't gay—at least I don't think so. It hit me, though, that Daddy can't have Dell back, not really, unless Daddy has some idea who Dell is and unless Carol can be a part of that reunion. Maybe, I thought, he is capable of enduring something potentially painful if it is a prerequisite to any possibility of having what he said, decisively and clearly, he wants.

Later that day, I tested the waters. While my husband and daughter were away and my mother was, as always, fetal and oblivious in the back bedroom, I maneuvered the conversation toward homosexuality. I tried to feel out his attitudes, to verify that he was open-minded on the subject. He confirmed. He told me the story of his gay neighbors. One of the men had died in a single car accident, hitting a pole after apparently falling asleep at the wheel one night. The other, his long-term partner, died the same way about three months later. In this story, there was empathy, recognition of the partners' love for each other and of the implications of the second death, and no hint of homophobia.

I tried to feel out whether he thought he might have a gay child. Nothing. My efforts only brought reference to his cousin, still unconfirmed, but almost certainly gay and apparently accepted by his parents. I was perplexed that he seemed completely unaware, but the idea stuck that there was work to be done. I had heard him.

I was scheduled to travel to Dell and Carol's in a month to teach a class at the university where Dell is a professor. I would tell Dell what Daddy had said. I would tell her that I intended to exercise the option she had long since given me to "out" her to him.

Dell heard me. She said it didn't matter what I did in that regard. She didn't, however, want Daddy to get any ideas that their estrangement was a result of her homosexuality and that, once he knew and said it was okay, all was well. Nothing would be any different, she said. "He cannot have me back," she said, "because he never had me." I said that I understood and that I would impress the point upon him. The conversation seemed to take a toll on Dell. I was hitting a sore spot. I was also violating some code of family dynamics, whereby I maintain my status as contact person for all only so long as I move no muscle ever toward engineering reunion.

At Thanksgiving, I was back in Florida. We got a sitter for my mother, and I coaxed Daddy to take his arthritic body to a mall food court with me where we would wait for my daughter and a neighbor girl outside the movie theater. With his hearing aid adjusted to hear me but not the masses, my father listened to the news, first slow in coming, then, on reading his reaction, faster and fuller, until he knew most everything, including that Dell is happily married to Carol.

He was absolutely surprised. He had never so much as thought of the possibility that Dell was gay. He thought I'd think it strange but, he said, he was glad: glad to know about Carol; glad to have some inkling of what Dell went through as a youth; glad to see many things through a new lens; glad to have some clue about his daughter's life; glad she is happy—glad in much the same way I had been glad more than a decade earlier.

I told him over and over that his and Dell's estrangement is not about her homosexuality; that nothing is different; that my revelation to him was inspired by his definitive "I want Dell back," and my belief that he could not have her back without knowing, but that knowing wouldn't bring her back. He understood so well that he was afraid to make a move toward her at all, but he asked me if it would be all right to send Dell and Carol a Christmas card. I said yes.

Daddy got a card back from "Dell and Carol," obviously signed by Carol. He mailed it to me for handwriting analysis, just to confirm it was not Dell's writing. It wasn't, but he was happy nonetheless. "I don't think Carol would have written it if Dell didn't say it was okay," he said. He said he thought he would like Carol and hoped they could meet.

That chance came unexpectedly and soon. In March, Mama rolled off the bed onto the carpeted floor and shattered her hip. Nine days later, with Daddy, Aaron, and me gathered around, she died a labored death. Dell was on the phone with me often in those nine days, interested in every detail. She and Mama spoke on my cell phone; I let her hear Mama breathing her last breaths before Daddy and Aaron arrived from the house. And I called her minutes after Mama stopped breathing, right there from Mama's hospital bed with Mama's still-warm hand in mine, to give her the news— that what should have happened eighteen years earlier, when Mama's massive stroke took her essence away from us; or in any event many years sooner, before so much suffering—what happened way too late—had finally happened much too soon, long before I was ready to let her go.

Dell and Carol came to the funeral in Alabama. They arrived minutes before the service and left shortly after. I had paved the way with the relatives and some others, and everyone was warm and welcoming of both. Dell, now forty-three, was quite apprehensive about coming into the church, wherein awaited high school teachers, old family friends and neighbors, and those suspected integrationist churchgoers from 1967. She had said she was coming for me. Then she said she was coming for her, that it was her mother's funeral and she wanted to be there. She hugged Daddy good-bye in that public forum and said, "Take care of yourself," and that was that. He loved those words, though, and he liked Carol very much.

I don't know if Daddy, with his bad heart, can live long enough for Dell to be ready to reconnect, or connect for the first time. She says she doesn't need to do it and that I should let it go. I've let it go, I guess, but I wonder if it might be in her best interest to have a father before he dies. He wasn't good at being a father when we were young; he didn't care to know any of us. I had to have a parent, however, and after we lost Mama, essentially, when I was just out of college, I persisted and persisted until I made him be my parent. He is a good father to me now. He listens and knows me, and we share a common history. I wish Dell could have a parent, too, and I wish she could feel affirmed in all of herself by reconnecting to those good values, traits, and roots that we all share, that came in part from Daddy in his better moments. I think that would have value for her, but I don't know, and she says it wouldn't. It is all up to Dell and Daddy now.

I don't really believe that Dell's being gay has nothing to do with their estrangement. I think that being gay permeates everything in a world weighted down by the unspeakable. What could in a perfect world be a fact of little importance is, in our world, at least the world in which Dell and I were formed, a fact that colors everything. So I believe that her having been unspeakably gay all those years is a central part of the fabric that estranged them. And in her reluctance to make amends with Daddy after his acceptance of her lifestyle, leading as it might to the impression that shame is what kept her away, Dell's being gay may be central to the stalemate that bars their reuniting.

For my own relationship with Dell, knowing she is gay has opened up a whole new level of interaction. Many of our conversations concern gay issues. Much of our time together is spent in ways it could not have been if I didn't know—in the company of Carol and their lesbian and gay friends and at lesbian clubs. Because of Dell's coming out, I now see lesbians where before there were none, I form friendships with lesbians, and I feel wonderfully reassured by these women's acceptance of me. Dell tells me it is okay for me to be as I am, that it is okay if I wear a skirt and heels in the company of lesbian women sporting cut-off jeans and old T-shirts. I laugh at and accept that I like to dress in drag. That doesn't mean I'm a bad girl, or a stupid sissy, or a traitor. It just means I am me, and I have a right to be me.

The Klan seems to have nearly died of natural causes. In workplaces people have learned not to say, and as a result maybe not so often to think, racist things. It is taboo openly to hate or use epithets about legislatively protected groups, but gay people are still fair game. We are stuck in 1967. Dell's coming out to me made me keenly aware of that and committed to do my small part to change it.

I am proud and amazed that Dell is out to the world. I do not understand how she can live with the ever-lurking possibility of violence. Of course, women live with it every day, like the air we breathe, having to be careful where we go when, and whether we are chaperoned by a protective male. But we have no real option to conceal our identity as women, and so we make no conscious choice to confront head-on the possibility of violence. By being out, as by writing a letter to the editor denouncing the Klan in 1964, Dell takes an affirmative step toward violent response. I do not think it would be tolerable to go on living without being out, for her, or for me in her shoes. So, like choosing to check into a hospital instead of dying yet, we do what we have to do.

Dell is an extraordinary person: talented, intelligent, and fun. She has found welcoming spaces and many friends in the world. Who she is has affected who I am in thousands of ways. Some of them have probably been to my detriment, but there are none that I would trade, and none that I can fully separate from the ways in

which the common threads running through our early lives entwined us both.

I am gratified that my child has been largely spared the unspeakable. She does not even comprehend the shame and fear that
Dell and I experienced. She loves her Aunt Dell and her Aunt
Carol and is proud of them both, together. She knows that they
love her, too, even if she does sometimes wear pink and high heels.

PART III:
ON HAVING A GAY BROTHER
AND A LESBIAN SISTER

18

The Puzzle

Brian Watts

Every year during Christmastime, for as long as I can remember, my family endeavors to put together a puzzle. We've tackled everything from a 1,000-piece Mickey Mouse, to a 500-piece picture of jellybeans, to 1,500-piece world monuments, to 750-piece works by favorite local artists. Like clockwork, on Christmas day, a folding table emerges from the depths of some forgotten closet and the family works steadily, over time, until a clear picture emerges and the last piece is pushed into place.

The task takes on a life all its own. Without much discussion the table goes up, commandeering the spotlight in the center of the living room or, as my niece calls it, "the do-nothing room." It really feels as though we are doing nothing; time would not pass so much as creep by. Eight in the evening becomes midnight in only a moment. Rarely is a chair empty. Family members never hover. It just seems that a substitute is always present when a spot is vacated, prompting a silent and clumsy exit followed by an awkward new arrival.

When I was younger, it was not uncommon to sneak off to bed around midnight, thinking that the house would soon be quiet and the day's labors put to rest, only to find the next morning that some unknown worker, who shunned sleep in favor of progress, had significantly furthered the project.

Even the most difficult puzzles were completed rather quickly—anywhere from Christmas day to shortly after New Year's. My mother purchased a special kit and glued each completed one to save as a monument to our industry. As with so many other arti-facts, these puzzles were soon laid to rest in the back of some stor-age closet, only to be happened upon in the heat of a frantic search for some long-forgotten, but suddenly urgently needed, treasure—their discovery ushering the smell of Christmas instantaneously.

Indeed, to me, puzzles represent family, holidays, and comfort. Though often frustrating, bordering on maddening, the Christmas puzzles were always approached with confidence. Experience taught us that, eventually, the task would be completed and the smell of glue would permeate the kitchen as my mother ensured that our struggle would not be forgotten.

I was a freshman in high school in 1991, in the heart of that ter-rible period when young people struggle to figure out who they are, who to emulate, and, with no small sense of desperation, fight to fit in.

I remember the night clearly, if not the exact date. It was a typi-cal, cold night in Provo, Utah. Snow draped itself across the ground like an inefficient blanket—able to cover, but not to warm. The house, on the other hand, was nearly too warm. That Christ-mas, five of the six children were home, two of them accompanied by spouses, and the body heat augmented the heat spewed by the furnace. My parents reigned over the chaos with seeming ease. The night was beginning to wane. We had been playing games for hours, occasionally paying a visit to the puzzle table to put in a quick piece, eating homemade nachos, and splitting colas. I was content, though already feeling the dread associated with the end of Christmas vacation. I had a friend over at the house, taking ad-vantage of the greatest Christmas gift of all: no school nights. On school nights, activities ended early and friends usually departed before night had fully taken hold. During Christmas break, the nights stretched on.

Then something odd happened. My father, without any effort at subtlety, suggested that we call it a night and hinted strongly that it was about time for my friend to depart. I looked at the kitchen clock. It was only ten and we were in the middle of a game, which quickly broke up without complaint. Our front door closed, shut-ting out the cold December air. My friend left with hurried whispers about plans for the next day. I walked back into the house and was called into my parents' room, along with two of my sisters. This was strange. In fact, I'm certain that such a gathering was unprecedented. Regardless, I joined what seemed to be a crowd on my parents' bed. I've forgotten most of the words that were said. The message my parents delivered, however, was clear: my older brother, Craig, the second of six children, was gay.

I've heard other people talk about the moment at which they learned that a close friend or loved one was gay. Many say that they weren't surprised. One couple even said that they had told their son that he was gay, quite a reversal from the usual situation. Me? I was completely shocked. It was as if two plus two suddenly equaled seven.

How could it be? How could my brother be the butt of all those locker-room jokes? How could my brother be one of those leather-clad freaks who marched down the streets of San Francisco? There had to be some mistake. I was staring straight down at my parents' bedspread. The pattern was memorized instantly and then slowly burned a permanent mark in my memory. It was as if I believed that if I stared at that pattern long enough, everything would make sense. My brother would be straight, the world would be black and white again, and, perhaps most important to a high school freshman, my family would be *normal*.

As confused as I was at that moment, some things began making a lot of sense. Craig was in his midtwenties, unmarried, and was not dating any women seriously—a situation encountered very rarely in Mormon culture, where most men are fathers before hitting the quarter-century mark. Beyond the obvious, what I had always thought of as my brother's quirks took on added significance and were in part explained by his sexual orientation. As I thought harder about the situation, I realized that my brother had always been different. It wasn't until then, however, that I caught a small glimpse of the explanation.

My father has since joked that he should have known that Craig was gay when he joined the Young Democrats Club at Provo High School. Located in the heart of Utah County, referred to affectionately by those of us in Salt Lake City as "The Compound," Provo was then and still is staunchly Republican. (A family friend once quipped that the prophet of the Mormon Church could run for office in Provo as a Democrat and still manage to lose.) Craig was an outstanding student, had been president of his class, and had participated in numerous extracurricular activities. He had graduated from Brigham Young University, moved on to a master's program at the University of Chicago, and was, at that time, pursuing yet another degree from Kyoto University in Japan. I was trying desperately to make the Craig I knew and the Craig I just found out about mesh to form a clear, coherent image.

All this time, my brain was in a crisis. I was racing through memories, making connections, and explaining what heretofore had been unexplained and unexamined facts. I was speechless and silent. My father had continued speaking to us after dropping the initial bombshell, but nothing he said seemed to reach me, his words just noise my brain was in no state to comprehend. What would my friends think? Do they know already? Do their parents? Should I tell them? How am I going to tell them? What about the church? What does this mean? I'm sorry to report that my most pressing concerns related almost solely to how this new information would affect me.

Even then, at that moment, I wasn't disgusted by or disappointed in my brother. I certainly wasn't proud or happy about his sexual orientation, but I knew that I loved him and I knew without question that my loyalty was properly placed with him. It's an odd thing, really. Growing up, the Mormon Church had bombarded me with the importance of FAMILY. Families are forever. Perhaps in this case, many members would feel that the teachings had backfired. I was confronted with a stunning conflict: reconciling love, loyalty, and homosexuality. Even now I'm surprised at how instantaneously I discarded the old notion: "Love the sinner. Hate the sin." As far as I was concerned, I was in a position where a choice had to be made, and I, perhaps ironically, perhaps not, chose my brother.

At that moment, however, "choosing my brother" had no content. There was no shape to the concept. Initially, "choosing him" meant not shunning him, not breaking off contact with him, and not being afraid of him. It did not mean hoping that he would find a partner and be in a loving relationship, and it did not mean discussing his orientation with anyone.

Finally, something my father said jarred me from my reverie and into the realization that it wouldn't be that easy. It wouldn't be acceptable, or perhaps even possible, to continue to live our lives as if my brother were either straight or a nonsexual being. My father said resolutely, "I want you to know that if Craig wanted me to march in a gay pride parade, I would walk right alongside him."

There was something especially potent about that statement which nearly stupefied me—something about the image it created: my father walking down a crowded street with my brother at his side; hundreds and hundreds of spectators lined up, pushing to get a better view of this parade that was taking place at some unknown time, in some unknown city; television cameras crowding the participants, hoping to capture the most provocative images to broadcast on the nightly news. There was something about this public willingness to be counted that shook me. The statement hurt—perhaps because I wasn't so sure I would be willing to do the same thing.

My father had purchased each of us copies of a book called *Peculiar People* (Schow, Schow, and Raynes, 1991). The book focused on the stories of Mormons who were dealing with homosexuality either in an abstract, academic and doctrinal manner or personally. When I returned to my room to go to sleep that night, I placed it under some clothes in my dresser, afraid that a friend might happen upon it if I left it in sight.

I was one of the last in my family to learn about my brother's sexuality. Two of my sisters had been present at the meeting, but one of them, Lori, had already formed a suspicion about Craig based on conversations with those family members in the know. As I was the youngest of the six children, it made a certain amount of sense that the information would be kept from me initially. I slowly discovered that Craig had been talking with my parents and some of my siblings for years before the fact trickled its way down. I was nevertheless a bit frustrated that I had been kept in the dark while the majority of the family had known about Craig for quite some time. I was also a bit upset that Craig had not told me himself.

Craig had not returned home for Christmas that year. He was living in Japan at the time and we rarely saw him. In fact, in many ways, Craig felt like a stranger to me. This was due in part to a significant age difference—Craig graduated from high school and began life in the "real world" when I was only seven years old. Almost immediately, he went to London for six months on a semester-abroad program run by Brigham Young University. Not too long after his return to Utah, he left on a two-year mission for the Mormon Church. He moved to Chicago soon after that, then to Japan, then to China. Due to our difference in age and Craig's globetrotting, I've come to know him primarily through visits and family vacations.

Because Craig lived thousands of miles away, it was often easy to sweep the issue of his homosexuality under the rug. It was not something I had to face on a daily basis, nor was it an issue that dominated my thoughts. As long as I could remain on the fence, quietly supportive but unwilling to stand up, I felt that I could get by.

Over the years, I've heard many people relate their own coming-out stories. Unfortunately, the majority of those stories involve some level of rejection or hatred from family members. In all honesty, I don't remember anyone in my family resenting or being angry with Craig. Mostly we were confused and sad. In many ways, I was like a deer in the headlights. I no longer participated in gay jokes at school. For the first time, I was listening to the words of the jokes and realizing how odd the whole phenomenon was. I began subtly pointing out to my friends that some great people were openly gay. In this respect, I drew heavily from the entertainment world, since I still believed that I didn't know anyone personally, other than my brother, who was gay. None of my friends ever doubted that some of our heroes were gay, but for some reason we had never made the connection between our hurtful joking and the individuals we respected. It was too easy to say that they were different from all the real gays—they were the exception to the rule. Our jokes were not about our gay heroes, but about the rest. For a while I drew the distinction myself: Craig was gay, but he was not one of *them*. This continued for a couple of years.

It's a cliché that once a family member comes out of the closet, the family goes in, but clichés are often based on truth, and my family was unquestionably in the closet. I don't know how long we would have stayed there if it hadn't been for an incident that turned our sorrow and confusion into anger and determination.

I had just returned home from hanging out with some friends when my sister Lori informed me that Craig had called from Japan to say he had been excommunicated from the Mormon Church. I was mad. The rest of my siblings were split between anger and sorrow. My mother was sad, and though we all felt betrayed, she was impacted the most severely by the tremendous hurt Craig's excommunication had caused. If my dad had feelings of sorrow, they were obscured by more powerful emotional states. He was livid *and* determined, an incredibly strong combination.

Everyone in my family, including my parents, had been born and raised in the Mormon Church. I am a sixth-generation Mormon. Given the church's relative youth, my ancestors joined early in its existence and then followed the church across the plains ultimately to settle in the West. Given this heritage, we were very active in church when I was growing up, which entailed a three-hour meeting every Sunday and activities once or twice during the week. My parents both accepted various callings, which required planning lessons, attending organizational meetings, and all manner of other activities that demanded a significant portion of their time. I didn't think it was odd. Only one family in our entire neighborhood was non-Mormon. Our family was no different from any other.

It was the extent of our dedication and our connection to the church that made Craig's excommunication such a tough pill to swallow. My mother, in particular, suddenly found it too difficult to attend the church meetings, which up to that point had been as much a part of life as breathing. This church, this organization, to which my family had given so much, had just kicked my brother to the curb. Making my anger rise even more, they had done this obviously hurtful act while claiming that their behavior was motivated by love.

I remember my dad talking to a family friend and saying, "If my son's not good enough for the church, then neither am I." That was a fair summation of the family's view at that time. We felt that we had been attacked. I firmly believe that Craig's excommunication was the best thing that ever happened to us. From my viewpoint, it represented a line being drawn in the sand, and it was the church that made our decision to stand by Craig seem so obviously correct. Family comes first—always.

Soon after the excommunication, we all became involved in Family Fellowship, a support group for Mormons dealing with homosexuality. I can still remember the first meeting we had in our living room. Close friends and other neighbors came and listened politely as issues were discussed, and then declined either overtly or implicitly ever to return to a meeting again.

Although many longtime friends were willfully oblivious to my family's participation in gay-related issues, a few seemed to sympathize with our efforts. I don't mean to say that they supported gay rights in any way, shape, or form. Rather, we got the sense that they understood what was motivating the activism. They were willing to tolerate these activities, so long as it was done without their involvement and so long as they were not dragged into the debate.

As friends put up barriers between the Family Fellowship group and themselves, others were coming out of the woodwork. I had no idea of the number of people who were coming to grips with this issue. Although our group began as a support for family members, it also became a safe place for gays and lesbians themselves. It was my involvement in the group that began to break down the barrier I had drawn between my brother and other gays and lesbians. The more gay and lesbian individuals I met, the more I realized the obvious: many are normal, well-adjusted, productive, and interesting members of every community.

It was during this time that the hard work was accomplished. My family was settling in and preparing its patience. Each day, the picture of our new reality and the roles that our values and principles would force us to play became clearer.

As the years snuck by, my siblings scattered around the globe, and I was soon the only bird left in the nest. My sister Lori is the second youngest in the family. Continuing a tradition that began with Craig, she had left Provo soon after high school graduation to live in London for several months as part of a semester-abroad program offered by Brigham Young University. Then she came home and transferred to a new school: Reed College in Portland, Oregon. I, along with my parents, accompanied her to orientation week. I found myself simultaneously envious of her opportunity to attend what can be described only as an eccentric, demanding, and fascinating college and nervous that, if the opportunity should present itself, I would not have the will to embark on such an adventure. Lori had switched tracks in a major way, shifting from one of the most conservative schools in the nation to one of the most liberal in a matter of months.

Of all my siblings, I was probably closest to Lori when I was growing up. As she is the fifth child and I am the sixth, we had several years together as the only children remaining under my parents' roof.

One night, it must have been late, I remember Lori and I were the only people awake in the house. Lori was back in town for an all-too-brief visit. We were each sitting on a kitchen barstool, engaging in what I thought were quick niceties before trudging off to bed. So I guess I was taken aback when she told me, seemingly out of the blue, that she felt she was a lesbian. I don't think I betrayed any outward evidence of my surprise, but I'm sure I hesitated before responding. I can't remember my exact words, but I said something such as "cool" or "all right," words that were affirmative, but not much beyond that.

I didn't act immediately on this latest revelation. I had been operating in a "don't ask, don't tell" mode up until that point. For some reason I didn't feel that informing my friends, all of whom knew about my brother's sexual orientation, about my sister was necessary. In retrospect, I think it may have been a secret desire that it wasn't true or that, as many family friends would later hypothesize, she was just "going through a phase," and that after she graduated from Reed, she'd settle down in our hometown with her old boyfriend, with whom I had enjoyed playing Ping-Pong.

It took awhile for me to accept fully Lori's sexual orientation. My resistance surprised me. By that point, I was attending virtually every Family Fellowship meeting and had also attended political rallies and marched in pride parades, but Lori's sexuality was rarely a topic of conversation. People knew about my brother, and it was easier just to stick with his story rather than add a new chapter. That I didn't exactly get along with the woman Lori was paired with at that time didn't help matters much.

A few years after Lori came out, I paid her a visit in San Francisco where she was then living. My girlfriend at the time and another good friend hopped in my car with a spring break to kill and absolutely no plans beyond knowing that my sister lived there and we could probably sleep at her place. I was lucky enough to arrive just at the time that Lori was beginning a new relationship, which is still flourishing nearly five years later. On that trip, I realized how much happier and more complete Lori was now that she had embraced her orientation.

I'd be lying if I said the seeming personality shift didn't lead to friction in the family. Lori, always the quiet and accommodating sibling, was starting to speak her mind and stick up for herself. It truly shook up the way our family pieced itself together. Lori has always been brilliant and witty and compassionate, but someone new was emerging. She seemed so much more confident, so much more in command of herself. Her quietness had transformed into assertiveness. She was no longer content to know silently the right answer; she had begun to tell us what the answer was. Her willingness to express her mind prodded my family into expanding its views on a variety of political and human rights issues. Once again, the picture we were attempting to fathom began to define itself further.

It's been over a decade since I first learned of my brother's sexual orientation and eight years since I've known about my sister's. Things seem easier to me now. Just like a puzzle, the more pieces that are in place, the easier it is to complete. I find myself no longer simply accepting Craig and Lori, but appreciating them, most often for qualities wholly unrelated to their orientation. I no longer hope that they'll someday settle down in Provo, be straight, and have 2.5 kids. I now sincerely hope that they will find and maintain happiness in a loving relationship. Just over three years ago I married a wonderful woman. Perhaps it took finding that happiness myself before I realized what a cruel thing it is to deny another human being of that rare opportunity.

It seems as if just yesterday I was staring at my parents' bedspread, trying to envision an appropriate and happy future, one that integrated love for family with a struggle for equal rights and acceptance. Without question, there have been difficult times, and I'm sure there will be more ahead. However, in retrospect, the creation of the present seems to have been effortless. My parents have become local celebrities in the gay community. Their efforts in the public and private spheres have impacted more lives than they will ever know. The rest of us contribute in our own ways. Still scattered around the world, it seems someone is always having a local impact somewhere.

Although our family has transformed drastically over the past decade, some things remain constant. Every Christmas, the card table still appears along with the latest addition to our puzzle collection, and, frequently, when I stumble into the living room after a good night's sleep and glance over at the table, I realize that someone has shunned sleep in favor of progress.

REFERENCE

Schow, R., Schow, W., and Raynes, M. (Eds.) (1991). *Peculiar people: Mormons and same-sex orientation.* Salt Lake City, UT: Signature Books.

Resources

ADDITIONAL READING

Bozett, F. W. and Sussman, M. B. (1989). Homosexuality and family relations: Views and research issues. *Marriage and Family Review, 14*(3/4), 1-8.

D'Augelli, A. R., Hershberger, S. L., and Pilkington, N. W. (1998). Lesbian, gay, and bisexual youth and their families: Disclosure of sexual orientation and its consequences. *American Journal of Orthopsychiatry, 68*(3), 361-371.

DeVine, J. L. (1984). A systemic inspection of affectional preference orientation and the family of origin. *Journal of Social Work and Human Sexuality, 2*(2/3), 9-17.

Gambaccini, P. (2001). The bond between brothers. In L. Siegel and N. L. Olson (Eds.), *Out of the closet into our hearts: Celebrating our gay/lesbian family members* (pp. 121-123). San Francisco: Leyland Publications.

Griffin, C. W., Wirth, M. J., and Wirth, A. G. (1986). *Beyond acceptance: Parents of lesbians and gays talk about their experiences.* Englewood Cliffs, NJ: Prentice-Hall, Inc.

Hauptman, L. (2001). Hineni. In L. Siegel and N. L. Olson (Eds.), *Out of the closet into our hearts: Celebrating our gay/lesbian family members* (pp. 138-139). San Francisco: Leyland Publications.

Herdt, G. and Koff, B. (2000). *Something to tell you: The road families travel when a child is gay.* New York: Columbia University Press.

Jones, C. R. (1978). *Understanding gay relatives and friends.* New York: The Seabury Press.

Kerr, M. E. (1986). *Night kites.* New York: HarperTrophy.

McKee, R. W. (2003). Moments of trust: Sibling responses to the disclosure of a sister's lesbian identity. Unpublished master's thesis. Richmond, VA: Virginia Commonwealth University.

Oswald, R. F. (2000). Family and friendship relationships after young women come out as bisexual or lesbian. *Journal of Homosexuality, 38*(3), 65-83.

Owens, R. E., Jr. (1998). *Queer kids: The challenges and promise for lesbian, gay, and bisexual youth.* Binghamton, NY: Harrington Park Press.

Pinol, M. (2001). Back to the bear world. In L. Siegel and N. L. Olson (Eds.), *Out of the closet into our hearts: Celebrating our gay/lesbian family members* (pp. 49-55). San Francisco: Leyland Publications.

Saffir, D. Z. (2001). Uncomfortable. In L. Siegel and N. L. Olson (Eds.), *Out of the closet into our hearts: Celebrating our gay/lesbian family members* (p. 58). San Francisco: Leyland Publications.

Strommen, E. F. (1989). Hidden branches and growing pains: Homosexuality and the family tree. *Marriage and Family Review, 14*(3/4), 9-34.

Strommen, E. F. (1989). "You're a what?": Family member reactions to the disclosure of homosexuality. *Journal of Homosexuality, 18*(1/2), 37-58.

Vargo, M. E. (1998). *Acts of disclosure: The coming-out process of contemporary gay men.* Binghamton, NY: Harrington Park Press.

Wersba, B. (1986). *Crazy vanilla.* New York: Harper & Row.

Weston, K. (1991). *Families we choose: Lesbians, gays, kinship.* New York: Columbia University Press.

Williamson, D. S. (1998). Disclosure is a family event. *Family Relations, 47,* 23-25.

ORGANIZATIONS

PFLAG (Parents, Families and Friends of Lesbians and Gays)
1726 M Street, NW Suite 400
Washington, DC 20036
Phone: (202) 467-8180
Fax: (202) 467-8194
www.pflag.org

COLAGE (Children of Lesbians and Gays Everywhere)
3543 18th Street #1
San Francisco, CA 94110
Phone: (415) 861-KIDS (5437)
Fax: (415) 255-8345
colage@colage.org
www.colage.org

Family Pride Coalition
P.O. Box 65327
Washington, DC 20035-5327
Phone: (202) 331-5015
Fax: (202) 331-0080
www.familypride.org

Order a copy of this book with this form or online at:

http://www.haworthpress.com/store/product.asp?sku=5283

SIDE BY SIDE
On Having a Gay or Lesbian Sibling

_____in hardbound at $29.95 (ISBN: 1-56023-464-4)

_____in softbound at $16.95 (ISBN: 1-56023-465-2)

Or order online and use special offer code HEC25 in the shopping cart.

COST OF BOOKS_____

POSTAGE & HANDLING_____
(US: $4.00 for first book & $1.50
for each additional book)
(Outside US: $5.00 for first book
& $2.00 for each additional book)

SUBTOTAL_____

IN CANADA: ADD 7% GST_____

STATE TAX_____
(NJ, NY, OH, MN, CA, IL, IN, & SD residents,
add appropriate local sales tax)

FINAL TOTAL_____
(If paying in Canadian funds,
convert using the current
exchange rate, UNESCO
coupons welcome)

☐ **BILL ME LATER:** (Bill-me option is good on
US/Canada/Mexico orders only; not good to
jobbers, wholesalers, or subscription agencies.)
☐ Check here if billing address is different from
shipping address and attach purchase order and
billing address information.

Signature_____

☐ **PAYMENT ENCLOSED: $**_____

☐ **PLEASE CHARGE TO MY CREDIT CARD.**

☐ Visa ☐ MasterCard ☐ AmEx ☐ Discover
☐ Diner's Club ☐ Eurocard ☐ JCB

Account # _____

Exp. Date_____

Signature_____

Prices in US dollars and subject to change without notice.

NAME_____

INSTITUTION_____

ADDRESS_____

CITY_____

STATE/ZIP_____

COUNTRY_____ COUNTY (NY residents only)_____

TEL_____ FAX_____

E-MAIL_____

May we use your e-mail address for confirmations and other types of information? ☐ Yes ☐ No
We appreciate receiving your e-mail address and fax number. Haworth would like to e-mail or fax special
discount offers to you, as a preferred customer. **We will never share, rent, or exchange your e-mail address
or fax number.** We regard such actions as an invasion of your privacy.

Order From Your Local Bookstore or Directly From
The Haworth Press, Inc.
10 Alice Street, Binghamton, New York 13904-1580 • USA
TELEPHONE: 1-800-HAWORTH (1-800-429-6784) / Outside US/Canada: (607) 722-5857
FAX: 1-800-895-0582 / Outside US/Canada: (607) 771-0012
E-mailto: orders@haworthpress.com

For orders outside US and Canada, you may wish to order through your local
sales representative, distributor, or bookseller.
For information, see http://haworthpress.com/distributors

(Discounts are available for individual orders in US and Canada only, not booksellers/distributors.)
PLEASE PHOTOCOPY THIS FORM FOR YOUR PERSONAL USE.
http://www.HaworthPress.com   BOF04